To:
_____

From:
_____

A Book for Grandad

A Book for Grandad

Geoff Tibballs

Michael O'Mara Books Limited

First published in Great Britain in 2010 by
Michael O'Mara Books Limited
9 Lion Yard
Tremadoc Road
London SW4 7NQ

Papers used by Michael O'Mara Books Limited are natural, recyclable
products made from wood grown in sustainable forests. The manufacturing
processes conform to the environmental regulations of the country of origin.

A CIP catalogue record for this book is available from the British Library.

ISBN: 978-1-84317-456-1

1 3 5 7 9 10 8 6 4 2

www.mombooks.com

Cover design, text design and typesetting by Ana Bjezancevic
Printed and bound in Great Britain by Clays Ltd, St Ives plc

*In memory of my
loving grandparents*

Contents

Introduction

You think you've got your life pretty much sorted: the kids have left home, the house is paid for and you've reached the age where nothing much can surprise or shock you.

Then along comes your first grandchild, and overnight your whole world is turned upside down by that innocent little bundle of joy. From that moment on, you find yourself wrapped around your grandchild's tiny fingers. The sticky stain on the expensive new carpet, the damage to your favourite garden plants, the broken model aircraft you have spent months labouring over – nothing matters if the perpetrator is your grandchild. You just smile and give them a warm, forgiving hug. It's what grandads do best.

Some children grow up without ever knowing their grandfathers. However, the fortunate ones who do get the opportunity to establish a relationship spanning two generations invariably carry with them for the rest

9

of their lives cherished memories of the unique bond that exists between grandchild and grandad.

It is a relationship that can be hugely beneficial to both parties. For the child, having a grandad is like acquiring a naughty big brother – except that you won't tell tales or take the last cookie out of the packet. For you, a grandchild provides the perfect excuse to turn the clock back fifty years. Who will be first in line for a go on little Johnny's new Nintendo Wii? Grandad, of course. It's just like being a dad again – but without the sense of responsibility. Being a grandad gives you a licence to run riot without fear of retribution, knowing that whatever mischief and mayhem you create will bring nothing worse than the familiar remark of 'Silly old Grandad!'

But grandads are more than just silver adolescents. As well as being a trusty playmate, you can take an active role in the development of your grandchildren, providing a sympathetic ear in times of trouble and dispensing words of wisdom based on your years of experience. For your part, you are happy to know that age is no bar to being useful and that you are now able to do all the things you had always wanted to do with your own children, but maybe just didn't have the time. In short, to become a grandad is to open a new, exciting and immensely rewarding chapter in your life story.

The best person in the world

THE RELATIONSHIP BETWEEN grandfather and grandchild is one of the most magical there is. No matter how strict or stressed a man might have been as a father, the arrival of his first grandchild transforms him into the most lovable, loving person in the world.

And children are aware of this incredible bond from the get-go: Grandad is patient, fun, cheeky and has a sweet tooth – he's simply the best person ever.

> 'The reason grandchildren and grandparents get along so well is that they have a common enemy.'
> SAM LEVENSON

Why grandads are great

❖ They have an endless supply of toffees.

❖ They love telling their grandchildren embarrassing stories about their parents, which can be stored in the memory for use at an appropriate time.

❖ They're big kids and relish every opportunity to do things Grandma disapproves of, particularly if it means racing down a snow-covered hill on a plastic shopping bag.

❖ They always make time to play with their grandchildren, especially when the washing up needs doing.

❖ They don't believe in healthy eating, and certainly won't expect the grandchildren to eat their Brussels sprouts.

❖ They were alive in the Olden Days.

❖ They are never as strict with their grandchildren as they were with their own children.

❖ The hair in their ears provides a constant source of fascination.

❖ They have an inexhaustible fund of stories.

❖ Most models come complete with a free grandma.

❖ They're beyond the age of caring about being told off and will willingly take the blame for any of their grandchildren's minor misdemeanours.

❖ When their granddaughter gets married, she only needs to find something new, something borrowed and something blue.

What makes a great grandad?

Grandchildren the world over know that grandads are wonderful, but every grandad has his own unique and memorable talents.

GRANDAD IN A MILLION

Nominating her grandad, Craig Hutton of Scottsdale, Arizona, for *Grand* magazine's 2008 Grandparent of the Year, five-year-old Ashley Fulbright wrote: 'He takes me to see horses, teaches me to floss my teeth, to use coupons, takes me to the zoo and plays, he gives the best hugs and is the best grandpa ever.'

Craig's daughter Lisa adds admiringly, 'My dad was meant to be a grandpa. His grandchildren love him to the moon.'

'The best place to be when you're sad is Grandpa's lap.'

ANON

KNIGHTED

In *Harry Potter and the Prisoner of Azkaban*, the third book in the ever-popular *Harry Potter* series, author J.K. Rowling named the conductor and driver of the Knight Bus – Stan Shunpike and Ernie Prang – in honour of her grandfathers, Stanley Volant and Ernie Rowling.

Bubble burst

'Grandad,' said his six-year-old grandson. 'You know something, you're just like God.'

'How's that?' asked Grandad, mentally polishing his halo.

The boy looked at him and said, 'You're both old.'

A GRATEFUL GRANDSON'S TRIBUTE

On being named GQ magazine's Man of the Year 2003, singer Justin Timberlake dedicated the award to his hero, his grandfather Bill Bomar, saying, 'He's my definition of a man.'

Timberlake said that, throughout the incredible highs of his career, he had remained grounded thanks to his grandpa's priceless advice: 'Always know where you're going and never forget where you came from.'

Grandad Bill sat in the audience with tears in his eyes and turned to his wife to say, 'I just love that boy so much.'

When Timberlake and his childhood friend Trace Ayala launched a clothing company in 2006, they named their company William Rast – a combination of Timberlake's grandfather's first name and Ayala's grandfather's surname. Timberlake explained, 'We just picked the two people who are most influential in our lives, and that's our grandfathers.'

> 'A grandfather is someone with silver in his hair and gold in his heart.'
> ANON

Grandad's snoring

While her parents were away on business, two-year-old Jennifer stayed at her grandparents' house and shared a room with them. To everyone's amazement, Grandad's incredibly loud snoring didn't even seem to bother her – in fact, it appeared to have a soothing effect.

About a week after returning home, Jennifer and her dad were in the back garden when somebody nearby started up a power saw. Jennifer's face immediately lit up.

'Grandpa!' she squealed.

OUT OF THE MOUTHS OF BABES

One Christmas, former US president Jimmy Carter took his family to Aspen, Colorado, where his good friend Prince Bandar of Saudi Arabia allowed them to use his luxurious mountaintop house. They were having breakfast there one morning when Carter's little grandson Jeremy asked, 'Papa, are you gonna die someday?'

Carter recalls, 'All grandparents want their kids

to love them so my heart just swelled up with pride that this kid was really worried about me, and I said, "Yes, Jeremy, everybody dies someday." I waited for him to say something else, but he didn't say anything. So eventually I said, "Why did you ask me that question?"

'He answered, "When you die, can we still come to Bandar's house?"'

'My grandfather is probably the most impressive person I know. He's Finnish, a very proud man, who would never take help from anybody. He came to America when he was a little boy, grew up during the Depression and sold shoes. He always used to tell us the story about getting a raise of three and a half cents, and how that was an incredible amount of success. He's extraordinary.'
MATT DAMON

Grandad/Grand dad

ONE OF THE greatest things about being a grandad is that you get to relive all the best bits of fatherhood – first words, birthday parties, learning to cycle – without having to bother with all the difficult aspects: teething, sleepless nights and temper tantrums. As soon as your grandchildren show signs of becoming bored or cranky, you can wrap things up and pack them off home.

Being a grandad is just like being a dad – only better!

Top 10 things about being a grandad

1. Even at sixty-plus, you can get away with behaving like a mischievous schoolboy again – but this time nobody tells you off.

2. You get to play with all the latest children's toys and gadgets.

3. Grandchildren are a great excuse to eat far too much ice cream.

4. If your grandchildren are little darlings, you take the genetic credit; if they're not, you can blame the parents.

5. You can tell your neighbours about how wonderful your grandchildren are – safe in the knowledge that they'll never know the truth.

6. Your grandchildren automatically assume you are wise, and – unlike your own children – will actually listen to what you have to say.

7. You get to answer tricky questions such as: Do fish sleep? How much does the sky weigh? What was the best thing *before* sliced bread?

8. Your grandchildren will often take pity on you and let you win at computer games.

9. The more grandchildren you have, the more opportunities you will have to go on 'It wasn't like this in *my* day' rants.

10. You have a whole new generation with whom to share unconditional love.

Like Dad, but cooler

Kane, aged twelve, says, 'My grandad is really cool. He's only forty-eight and rides in leather on his motorbike! Plus he knows how to use all the latest gadgets and stuff. He's like a second dad to me.'

Second dad

For a variety of reasons, grandads can often end up being more influential in a child's life than dads. The following stories show the importance of grandads' parental expertise on a number of celebrities.

ROOFTOP TALES

Following the divorce of his parents when he was just two years old, Al Pacino was effectively raised by his grandfather.

'He didn't talk much,' says Pacino. 'He wasn't demonstrative. He didn't display his feelings much in terms of affection. But he was there ... I used to love to hear him tell me stories about what it was like in New York in East Harlem in the early 1900s. He would just string these yarns for hours on the roof. I would spend nights up there, him talking to me. It's almost like a grandfather and grandson on a fishing boat, but we were in the South Bronx, up on a roof.'

> 'Being grandparents sufficiently removes us from the responsibilities so that we can be friends.'
> ALLAN FROME

LEADING BY EXAMPLE

As a young boy, Bill Clinton lived with his grandparents. He loved going to work with 'Papaw' – as he called his grandfather James Eldridge Cassidy – at his two jobs, running a small grocery store and working as a night watchman at a sawmill. Clinton later attributed his grandfather with being the first male influence in his life: as well as teaching Bill to read by the age of three, this 'incredibly kind and generous man' would share his life experiences with his grandson.

In his autobiography *My Life*, Clinton wrote, 'I loved spending the night with Papaw at the sawmill. We would take a paper bag with sandwiches for supper, and I would sleep in the backseat of the car. My grandfather loved working there, too. Except for the time Papaw closed the car door on my fingers in the dark, those nights were perfect adventures.'

Reflecting on Papaw's unexpected role as a father figure, Clinton added, 'He loved Mother and me more than life. His love, and the things he taught me, mostly by example, including appreciation for the gifts of daily life and the problems of other people, made me better than I could have been without him.'

A WATCHFUL EYE

David Beckham has never forgotten the debt he owes to his grandad, Joseph West. It was football-mad Joseph who set Beckham on the road to stardom in 1986, paying £125 to send the eleven-year-old to a football school, where he caught the eye of scouts from Manchester United.

'How can I thank him enough?' asked Beckham. 'It turned out to be the defining moment in my career.'

When Beckham collected his OBE from the Queen in 2003, he invited his grandad to be at his side.

'I was so close to my grandad,' said Beckham after Joseph's death. 'He was so proud of everything in my career and he followed every game. He would call me after every game, every training session and all through my career. He watched nearly all of my early games and I liked him being there. He was softer with me than Dad when it came to talking about the match and how I'd played.'

'One of my earliest memories is of sitting on my grandfather's shoulders and watching the astronauts come to shore in Hawaii. I remember the cheers and small flags that people waved, and my grandfather explaining to me: "This is what America's all about; we can do anything when we put our minds to it."'
BARACK OBAMA

Five ways to win over a grandchild

1. Tell the kind of puerile jokes that only young children and grandads find funny.

2. Ask them all about their projects and trips, friends and enemies, and let them know that you're always interested in what they have to say.

3. Make them laugh by recounting all the naughty things you used to do as a boy.

4. Be firm but fair – don't let them get away with bad behaviour but don't overreact when they (inevitably but accidentally) smash something.

5. Teach them lots of useful life skills, such as tying knots, wiring plugs and hiding peas under mashed potato.

Just a big kid

EVEN THE OLDEST and most sensible grandads – the ones who can't tolerate 'that racket' or understand 'the youth of today' – occasionally forget their austerity and reveal themselves to be big kids at heart. Whether it's joining in with a children's game, telling puerile jokes or watching Disney cartoons in wide-eyed amazement, there's no doubt there's a young boy inside every old boy!

> 'Grandparents are there to help the child get into mischief they haven't thought of yet.'
> GENE PERRET

Emergency repairs

When Sir Winston Churchill visited President Eisenhower in the White House in 1959, Eisenhower's eight-year-old granddaughter Susan interrupted the conversation to inform the two statesmen that her doll's nappy had fallen off. Without batting an eyelid or breaking off the dialogue, Churchill fixed the doll's attire and returned her to her delighted owner.

Political priorities

When Barack Obama tried to reach Senator Joe Biden to ask him to run for Vice President, Biden wasn't in Washington waiting by the phone – he was at his granddaughter Maisey's eighth birthday party in Wilmington, Delaware. After Maisey blew out the candles and the cake was cut, Biden told the family gathering about his phone call with Obama. While the rest of the family cheered and hugged, Maisey went up to him and asked simply, 'Pop, can I have more ice cream cake?'

At the subsequent Democrat Party convention, Biden recalls how another of his granddaughters,

Finnegan, came up to him, grabbed him by the coat and said excitedly, 'Malia and Sasha [Obama] and I want to have a sleepover!'

'The next thing we know,' says Biden, 'we're clearing out a hotel room at the convention and putting down mats and ordering up pizza and movies! When I walked in, looked around the room and saw those kids together, I knew I'd made the right choice.'

A crafty ruse

One thing grandads seem to enjoy more than anything else is teasing their grandchildren when they are little. For years, one grandad had his grandson believing that, when an ice cream van plays its chimes, it was to let children know they had no ice cream left.

Money for nothing

When comedian Vic Reeves was a boy, he and his family would visit his grandparents in their Yorkshire bungalow every few weekends.

Grandad was a delightfully eccentric fellow who

was addicted to gadgets, and on one summer holiday he brought along a metal detector and let his grandchildren take turns in combing the beach while he monitored their progress from the chalet roof with a pair of World War Two binoculars.

That enterprise yielded a number of coins dropped by holidaymakers, but another of Grandad's money-making schemes was even more imaginative. In Reeves's autobiography *Me: Moir* (his real name is Jim Moir), he wrote, 'It involved me wearing a sheet and towel wrapped around my head. I was told to walk up and down the chalets, clutching a small tin bowl, and saying that I was a poor Arab boy in dire need of money for food. This I duly did, and thoroughly enjoyed it, especially when I returned home with my pot brimming.'

Joker in the pack

A seven-year-old girl from Burnett, Wisconsin, called the police in 2007 – because she thought her grandad was cheating in a family game of cards. When officers arrived to investigate, they were told that the girl had just learned how to dial 911. It was not clear whether or not Grandad had actually been cheating.

> 'It's funny what happens when you become a grandparent. You start to act all goofy and do things you never thought you'd do. It's terrific.'
> MIKE KRZYZEWSKI

A child in the White House

Three-year-old Curtis Roosevelt and his older sister Eleanor went to live in the White House shortly after their grandfather Franklin D. Roosevelt became president in 1933. FDR was a devoted grandfather – so much so that Undersecretary of the Treasury Dean Acheson later complained that it was often impossible to get the president to focus on affairs of state during breakfast meetings in his bedroom, because he preferred to lark around with his grandchildren.

'Every morning after breakfast,' recalls Curtis, 'my sister and I were escorted to my grandfather's second-floor bedroom. He would immediately halt his discussions with the aides assembled around his bed and direct all his attention to us. He wasn't just the president of the United States, he was a terrific grandfather. He always had time for me.'

Treasured memories

Hannah O'Byrne from New Zealand thinks the world of her grandad, Dick Anderson.

'My grandad is extremely special to me,' she says. 'He is great at making things. He made a petrol station for my brother and cousins to keep and play with their cars. He also built little tunnels and bridges. Then we all got to help paint them. It was really fun. Grandad always has stories about when he was a boy; he is a very useful asset when it comes to school projects! Whenever I come to visit, I am always bombarded with food. I treasure my grandad a lot. He is the best.'

> 'I like to do nice things for my grandchildren – like buy them those toys I've always wanted to play with.'
> GENE PERRET

Staying with Grandad

IF YOU LIVE close enough to your grandchildren to be able to babysit, you can guarantee that your children will take every opportunity to ask you to do just that! Whether you go to their house or they come to yours, you'll find that babysitting your grandchildren provides a wonderful excuse for getting to know them a little better.

There are few things more lovely than being the last person your grandchildren see at night, tucking them in and reading them a story before turning out the lights.

Babysitting FAQs

Although you're perfectly capable of looking after young children – you've done it before – the idea of being in sole control of somebody else's children can be rather daunting. These FAQs should help ease your fears.

WHAT SHOULD I FEED THEM?

The quick answer is: keep it simple. For some recipe ideas, as well as ways in which you can involve your grandchildren in the meal preparation, turn to p.70.

WHAT TIME SHOULD THEY GO TO BED?

If you've babysat your grandchildren before, you'll know that asking them what time they normally go to bed will result in an outright lie. Ask their parents beforehand and find out if they have any other bedtime rituals – reading stories, leaving a light on or the door ajar, etc. For some suggestions of nice books you might read together, turn to p.39.

HOW DO I ENTERTAIN THEM?

Fortunately, there's no need to rush out and buy a computer console or other new-fangled gadget. Children expect a tamer, more traditional sort of entertainment at Grandad's, and should be easily distracted by fast-paced board or card games (Ludo, Uno, KerPlunk, Jenga, Guess Who?). Alternatively, if they insist on watching a DVD, you could introduce them to older sitcoms – *'Allo 'Allo*, *Fawlty Towers*, *Blackadder* – which are surprisingly popular with young kids. You'll have them clamouring to be babysat by Grandad more often!

Final warning

While babysitting, Grandad was playing trains with his grandson. The boy was in a mischievous mood, however, and was intent on pulling the cat's tail. After three warnings had gone unheeded, Grandad finally told him firmly to stop. His grandson immediately went over to him, head bowed, lower lip quivering, and said, 'Grandad, I still love you but if you talk to me like that again, you may not be able to play with my train set anymore.'

> *'My grandchild has taught me what true love means. It means watching Scooby-Doo cartoons while the basketball game is on another channel.'*
>
> GENE PERRET

Do's and don'ts of babysitting

The reason why grandparents usually come as a pair is because the laws of childcare state that it requires a minimum of four hands to control the average two-year-old.

There are, however, occasions when unforeseen circumstances (such as not being able to think up an excuse in time) leave poor Grandad having to undertake babysitting duties alone. Suddenly you know how Daniel felt just before he was thrown into the lions' den. It's tough enough looking after one child, but with two or more, you can guarantee that they will conspire against you. But if there are tantrums and tears, try not to worry: you'll calm down when you get home.

DO...

❖ Learn the names of your grandchildren's favourite toys. You may never be forgiven if you get one wrong.

❖ Establish from the outset whether you will be required to take part in energetic games. If you're hoping for a quiet evening, you may need to produce a medical certificate or a note from Grandma.

❖ Wear clothes whose appearance may even be enhanced by being smeared with peanut butter, ice cream or chocolate.

❖ Confirm exactly what time the children have to be in bed and make sure they know it, too. A vague timetable will simply lead to repeat requests to stay up for an extra half-hour, and before you know it you'll all be sitting up together watching the midnight horror movie.

❖ Make sure you have a phone number for Mum or Dad in the event of an emergency – after checking that they haven't secretly packed their bags with a view to fleeing the country, that is.

❖ If your charges are young, practise your nappy-changing skills beforehand because you will probably be a little rusty. A child with two legs in the same hole is a sign of this.

DON'T...

❖ Have a stiff drink at the start of the evening to calm your nerves. You'll need all your wits about you for the battle ahead.

❖ Arrive at the last minute, otherwise the parents will be in a hurry to leave and you may never find out where the baby wipes are kept. Curtains are no substitute.

❖ Take out your frustrations on Teddy.

'I do less globe-trotting now because we've got our first grandson, and he's wonderful. I miss him when I go away – it's so soppy, isn't it? I see him as often as possible – at least twice a week. There is that thing with your first grandchild. It's something very special. I feel I am lucky to have a strong relationship with him and watch him grow up and not be distant.'

MICHAEL PALIN

The patient babysitter

Absolutely Fabulous actress June Whitfield has only the fondest memories of her maternal grandfather. She says he was a 'most patient babysitter' who would uncomplainingly answer endless calls for a glass of water or some other excuse when she was really supposed to be asleep.

June's room was connected to her grandparents' room by a door, which would always be left ajar when Grandad was on babysitting duties. One night, puzzled by strange hissing sounds that were emanating from Grandad's room, June's curiosity finally got the better of her and she crept to the door for a closer look. There she found him reading the newspaper, smoking his pipe and occasionally spitting, with remarkable accuracy, into the gas fire.

Puppy love

Donny Osmond, who inexplicably has become old enough to be a grandfather since his 1970s heyday, loves to babysit his young grandson Dylan. Indeed, the boy has captivated him ever since his birth.

'As soon as I heard the first cry we were just outside the delivery room, and the next thing I see is my son walking out with the baby in his arms. Here's my twenty-four-year-old son and he looks at me and says, "This is my son." To see your little baby say that about his baby is a powerful moment.'

Donny says that, as a grandfather, he doesn't feel the responsibility of the teaching process, just the loving process.

'You love him and then you send him home. You worry about him and everything, but it's a whole different kind of concern. Because it's not your full responsibility, you just have all the good stuff.'

When it comes to putting Dylan to bed, his parents know they can rely on Grandpa Donny.

'I just start singing and rocking him with a kind of melody I came up with and which I sang to all my kids. And it just pops out as I'm rocking him in my arms. And I'm able to put Dylan to sleep just like that.'

> 'By the time the youngest children have learned to keep the house tidy, the oldest grandchildren are on hand to take it to pieces.'
> CHRISTOPHER MORLEY

Books at bedtime

As WELL AS providing an opportunity to spend precious time together, a bedtime story helps young children to settle down for the night – as long as you don't choose anything too scary. Reading to your grandchildren will also give you a great excuse to show off your talent for silly accents and funny voices.

'My grandfather was a clergyman, a Church of England rector in a parish in Norfolk. I spent a lot of my childhood in his household, because my father died when I was seven. Grandpa was a very good, old-fashioned country clergyman and a wonderful storyteller, too.'
PHILIP PULLMAN

Story time with Grandad

Celebrated author Roald Dahl made his granddaughter
Sophie the heroine of his best-selling book *The BFG*,
the tale of a lonely girl (called Sophie) who befriends
a giant.

Actress and model Sophie Dahl remembers, 'I
spent huge amounts of time with my grandfather and
adored him, absolutely adored him. He used to pin up
the short stories I sent him as a child on the walls of his
writing hut. He was always telling us stories in fragments
– sometimes after they had been written or on other
occasions while the idea was still being germinated. For
me, that was nothing out of the ordinary. It was only
when I had friends come to stay, and I saw how excited
they all got, that I picked up on this being something
that other people saw as special.'

Stories for all occasions

A number of factors will dictate which story you decide to
read to your grandchildren: their ages, interests, reading
level and whether or not they're easily frightened. Keep
the story fairly short – a short story or a chapter of a

novel – otherwise you'll end up keeping the children awake for hours after their bedtime.

But what to read? Here are some suggestions.

CLASSICS

You could try some of these favourites, old and new. Don't worry: you won't be expected to read the entire book in one sitting!

Harry Potter by J. K. Rowling
The Tale of Peter Rabbit by Beatrix Potter
The Cat in the Hat by Dr Seuss
Thomas the Tank Engine by Rev. W. Awdry
Black Beauty by Anna Sewell
The Gruffalo by Julia Donaldson
Charlie and the Chocolate Factory by Roald Dahl
The Story of Tracy Beaker by Jacqueline Wilson
The Borrowers by Mary Norton
How the Grinch Stole Christmas by Dr Seuss
The Wind in the Willows by Kenneth Grahame
The Very Hungry Caterpillar by Eric Carle

A lesson learned

Whenever he was babysitting his three-year-old granddaughter, Grandad loved to read picture stories to her, to help with her education. One evening, he decided to test her on her colours by pointing to pictures in her reading book. Whichever colour he asked, she would give the correct answer: blue, green, red, orange, brown, purple, yellow – she knew them all. Grandad was really impressed and continued with the game throughout the rest of the book. When all the colours on the last page had been picked out and identified, the child turned to Grandad with a look of grave disappointment and said, 'You know, Grandad, you really should try to figure out some of these yourself.'

MAKE IT UP AS YOU GO ALONG

If you want to tell your grandchildren a story they've never heard before, make up your own as you go along! All you need to get you started is a main character – a child not unlike your grandchild would be ideal – and a noteworthy event. Perhaps the character could sneak into a museum or zoo at night, or join the circus, or discover a magical talent. If you get stuck, ask your grandchild what the character should do next, and you'll end up telling the story together.

If you're nervous about thinking up something funny on the spot, you could write a short story during the week, one involving your grandchild and other family members getting into exciting adventures and amusing scrapes.

TELL IT AGAIN, GRANDAD

When you're plumbing the depths of your imagination for a new and unique bedtime story, why not draw on your own experiences? Grandchildren love to hear about all the funny, naughty or daring things Grandad did 'in the Olden Days' – and the more historical you can make your childhood or career sound, the better. A few choice reminiscences about a world without iPods, text messages and emails will have your grandchildren as wide-eyed in disbelief as the most outlandish fairy tale.

It's the way
I tell them

WHAT IS IT with grandads and terrible jokes? As a rule, Grandad's jokes have to be among the oldest, corniest one-liners around – and yet there's something about the way his boyish eyes light up as he reels out the same old clangers that makes them charmingly silly. And let's face it: when it comes to sharing cracker jokes at Christmas, there's no one better than Grandad to do them justice!

> *'I'm very proud of my gold pocket watch. My grandfather, on his deathbed, sold me this watch.'*
> WOODY ALLEN

I say, I say, I say

Here are some examples of classic grandad humour. But be warned: with familiarity these one-liners will eventually induce more groans than laughter.

❖ What's the difference between a mailbox and a dog? You don't know? Well, I won't ask you to post a letter, then!

❖ What has four legs but can't walk? A table.

❖ Which is faster: hot or cold? Hot: you can catch a cold.

❖ Why did the tomato blush? Because he saw the salad dressing.

❖ Why did the baby raspberry cry? Because his mother was in a jam.

❖ What do you get if you cross an elephant with a fish? Swimming trunks.

❖ Why do lions eat raw meat? Because they don't know how to cook.

❖ What lies at the bottom of the ocean and shakes? A nervous wreck.

❖ What do you get if you cross a cow with a grass cutter? A lawn mooer.

❖ Why is getting up at five o'clock in the morning like a pig's tail? It's twirly.

❖ What do you call a donkey with three legs? A wonkey.

❖ Did you hear about the grape that got crushed? It gave out a little wine.

❖ What's smelly, round and laughs? A tickled onion.

❖ Why do hummingbirds hum? Because they don't know the words.

❖ What's yellow and dangerous? Shark-infested custard.

❖ What do you get if you cross a sheep and a kangaroo? A woolly jumper.

❖ What do you call a man with a banana in his ear? Anything you like: he can't hear you.

❖ How do you keep an idiot in suspense? I'll tell you later.

Old yarns

As well as their trademark one-liners, grandads are renowned for their skill at spinning cheesy yarns – the sort of jokes that really ought to be followed by a cabaret-style comedy drum roll.

GO SLOW

Grandad was driving along the motorway at his usual speed of about 20mph. As other cars flashed past, sounding their horns, a policeman pulled Grandad over and said, 'I expect you know why I stopped you, sir.'

'Sure do,' replied Grandad. 'I was the only one you could catch!'

PAINFUL JOKE

Grandad was distraught to see his eight-year-old granddaughter break her arm in a fall in his garden, but he did his best to keep her spirits up. When the doctor had finished examining the child's arm, Grandad asked solemnly, 'Doctor, will she be able to play the piano?'

'Oh yes,' replied the doctor, 'she'll definitely be able to play the piano.'

'That's amazing!' cried Grandad, 'Because she couldn't play it before!'

'I always give my grandkids a couple of quarters when they go home. It's a bargain.'
GENE PERRET

A WARY WIT

Coming from a poor background, Robert Redford's grandfather always worried that acting was a financially risky profession and that young Robert would never have enough money. Even when Redford began enjoying considerable success as a movie star, Grandad couldn't help but express his reservations.

Redford remembers visiting him at a nursing home in Connecticut.

'I wanted to please him, so I got dressed up and pulled up in a fancy car and told him, "Things are going great. I got this part and that part." The nurses had fallen in love with my grandfather because he was a real charmer, and they said, "Charles, isn't it lovely your grandson is doing so well?"

'And he said, "Yeah, but you might want to count the silverware when he leaves."'

CONFUSING SIGNALS

Grandad was driving Grandma home late one night when he stopped alongside another car at a red traffic light. He immediately turned to the driver of the other car and started waving and pointing frantically, a look of manic excitement on his face.

Seeing Grandad's wild gestures, the driver started to panic. He checked that the doors were properly closed and that there were no warning lights on the dashboard. Convinced that something must be seriously wrong with his car even though he had only owned it for a couple of months, he stepped out to check the tyres.

As he did so, the traffic light changed to green and Grandad drove off, calling out cheerfully as he departed, 'That's our old car. Make sure you take good care of her!'

That's show business!

A GREAT TRANSFORMATION occurs in a man as soon as he becomes a grandfather. It's not the grey in his hair or the false teeth in the bathroom, but rather the overwhelming compulsion to clown about. It seems there are few things Grandad loves more than entertaining his grandchildren with wild stories, laughably unfunny jokes and boisterous games. The more grandchildren he has, the more experienced a showman Grandad becomes!

Rehearsed routine

Being a grandad is often like being a full-time entertainer. That's why grandads have their favourite little jokes and routines. One grandson remembers that, whenever his grandparents had a meal at his parents' house, Grandad would nudge Grandma and say, 'It's nice here, isn't it? Are they open on Sundays?'

Put your hands together for ... Grandad!

Time spent with your grandchildren is precious, particularly if you live far away and only see them once or twice a year. Children are easily bored and distracted, though, so keeping them entertained is definitely the best way to make a family visit a memorable few days.

Entertaining grandchildren comes naturally to grandads once they get into the swing of things, but if you're a first-time grandad or haven't had to deal with children since your own were young, you might find these suggestions helpful. They're all designed to strengthen the special bond between you and your grandchildren, with minimum damage to your home, wallet or sanity.

SLEEPOVER

All children love sleepovers, so you'll be onto a winner as soon as you suggest hosting one. But the key to organizing a successful sleepover – one that won't leave your nerves in tatters – is forward planning. Invite as many of your grandchildren as you can manage and prepare some party food, but rather than sit the kids down with a DVD – which they can just as easily watch at home – draw up a list of games that you can all play together.

Here are a few tips for a successful slumber party:

❖ Alternate more boisterous games such as 'Musical Chairs' with sitting-down games such as 'Pass the Parcel' or 'I Spy', so that neither they nor you get too exhausted too soon.

❖ Don't organize a running-about game immediately after the food or you could end up with a hefty carpet-cleaning bill.

❖ Give a small prize to the winner of each game.

❖ Curb your competitive instincts at 'Pin the Tail on the Donkey' to make sure that everyone wins a game.

❖ Once the children are tucked into their sleeping bags on your lounge floor, leave the lights dimmed for half an hour before switching off completely. This will give the kids a chance to wind down and talk quietly among themselves.

❖ Don't worry if they're so excited that they don't want to go to bed early. With any luck it means they'll sleep later the next morning, allowing you a well-deserved lie-in.

After spending the night 'sleeping rough' on your lounge floor, your grandchildren will return home having enjoyed a great adventure that they will remember fondly for years to come.

VARIETY SHOW

Put on a variety show with your grandchildren. It doesn't have to be a grand spectacular – a fifteen-minute show performed in your own home in front of the rest of the family will do. Combine your grandchildren's talents – maybe singing, dancing, playing a musical instrument, doing impressions, joke-telling or reading – with your own. There can be solo spots for your grandchildren as well as joint comedy routines, which will be all the more appealing if they involve dressing up. Rehearsals for your show will be a fun way of spending time together.

One thing to remember, though: if your grandchild is a budding gymnast, remove any precious ornaments from the room – just in case.

> *'If I had known that grandchildren were going to be so much fun, I would have had them first.'*
> BILL LAURIN

STORYTELLING

Few pastimes better present the opportunity for spending quiet, quality time together than storytelling. You can either choose one of your grandchild's favourite stories to read or recount some adventures from your own life, with funny voices and actions of course, which will help bring you closer together. Don't forget to let your grandchildren demonstrate their newly acquired reading ability to you – there's probably nobody they'd rather show off to than their grandad.

PAINTING

Young children in particular love to paint, but since it could be asking for trouble to let them loose with a tin of emulsion on your dining room walls, your best way of catering to their enthusiasm is to use water colours on a sheet of paper. If it's a nice day, you could both go out into the garden or to a park and paint the same view. Or you could stay indoors and paint faces on hard-boiled eggs. Shared experiences are invariably the best.

For the most authentic painting experience, wear tunics, artistic berets and drawn-on moustaches.

> 'When I was little, my grandfather used to make me stand in a closet for five minutes without moving. He said it was elevator practice.'
> STEVEN WRIGHT

GET GLUING

If your grandchild enjoys making models, the pair of you can join forces in assembling a model aeroplane or ship. This will occupy you both for hours – even longer if you accidentally glue your hands together.

(As a grandad, you will have to pretend at least once during the model-building that you actually *have* glued your hands together…)

X MARKS THE SPOT

Devise a treasure hunt. Hide toys or sweets around the house or garden and write a series of clues to help the children find them. This will encourage them to exercise and think for themselves in a fun way, and it's a great excuse to buy an extra-large bag of sweets.

If you're feeling particularly creative, make pirate hats for everyone out of pieces of cardboard.

DRESSING UP

To ring the changes, why not combine a selection of favourite board games with improvised activities such as 'shops', 'hospital', or 'school', which will give your grandchild the opportunity to be inventive and indulge in role playing? 'Hospital' is particularly popular with granddaughters, but be ready to hear some alarming diagnoses – and, of course, for the sake of realism, be prepared for a long wait before you are seen.

'Our kids really enjoy hanging out with my parents, and there's this wonderful back-and-forth. My dad [actor Jerry Stiller] will tell stories and do characters. He loves being a grandfather, but he doesn't want to be called "Grandpa". My kids call him Mr Kineeche. I don't know why – they make up silly names and they stick. So when he comes over, he announces himself – "Mr Kineecheee is heeeere!" – in some weird accent.'
BEN STILLER

THE EAGLE HAS LANDED

Devise a secret code of communication between you and your grandchild. Simply by using numbers to represent the letters of the alphabet, removing vowels from words or writing words backwards, you can create seemingly mysterious codes that will pander to your grandchild's inner spy. Best of all, only the two of you will be able to understand them. You can also try writing secret messages with a white wax crayon on white paper. When covered with thin paint, the message magically appears.

If you can rope in Grandma or another adult to plant some secret messages and 'evidence' around the house and garden, you and your grandchild can communicate via walkie-talkie as you get to the bottom of whatever mystery you've concocted.

HAPPY SNAPPERS

Photography is a lovely hobby for grandads and grandchildren to share. Not only does it get you all out of the house and into the fresh air, but it will also help your grandchildren to appreciate nature and their surroundings. Modern digital cameras for children are built to withstand hard knocks and they provide instant results without the boring seven-day wait for your photos to be developed at the pharmacy.

Perhaps take a trip to a local zoo and get photos of you both doing your best monkey impressions in front of the baboon enclosure.

START A COLLECTION

Since children love collecting things, suggest starting up a collection from scratch. You can either choose something relatively straightforward and inexpensive that you can go off and buy together at the shops – such as postage stamps or badges – or think of something slightly more unusual, such as unusual feathers or buttons.

Remember to ask your grandchildren's parents for approval first, however: while they might make their peace with a house full of pencil sharpeners, they may draw the line at housing the national collection of glass eyes.

Shark practice

Grandad's favourite party piece was to ask his grandchildren, 'Do you want to see my man-eating-shark impression?'

When they said yes, he'd go, 'Mmmm. This shark tastes good!'

That's Magic!

Australian choreographer and *Strictly Come Dancing* judge Craig Revel Horwood reveals in his autobiography *All Balls and Glitter* how his grandad Mozza used to dress up as a clown for children's parties and perform

59

magic tricks. One trick always had young Craig baffled.

'He used to tell me that if you placed your hands on someone's temples, you could read minds, and I was totally sucked in by this. He would say, "Think of a number between one and ten," and then guess what it was by putting his hands on our heads.'

Hugely impressed, Craig hoped this incredible talent would rub off on him and constantly went around putting his hands on people's temples, but he seemed not to have the magic touch. Was Grandad a mind reader after all?

Birthday Greetings, Bottle of Wine

In 2006, for Sir Paul McCartney's sixty-fourth birthday, his daughters Mary and Stella sneaked his three grandchildren – Arthur, Elliott and Miller – into the famous Abbey Road Studios in London, where they recorded their own version of the Beatles' song 'When I'm Sixty-Four' as a present.

Grandad knows best

SOMEWHERE ALONG THE way from being a bewildered young dad to being a wise old grandad, a man mysteriously gains an awful lot of profound and often surprising knowledge, all of which can be dispensed to his grandchildren in weekly chunks of advice.

Advice from Grandad always seems so much more heartfelt and relevant than advice from other people.

'My grandfather gave me the best career advice ever. He said, "Never miss an opportunity to just shut up."'
REESE WITHERSPOON

Grandad's top 20 pieces of advice

Grandad's little maxims about everyday life can sometime sound foolish – but they inevitably turn out to make perfect sense. If you're not the sort of grandad who's used to doling out advice, try these typical statements for size:

❖ Never argue with a fool, in case people can't tell you apart.

❖ Don't pick an argument with someone who's packing your parachute.

❖ Never stand between a dog and a fire hydrant.

❖ When your dad is angry and asks you, 'Do I look stupid?' – don't answer.

❖ Never be too full for dessert.

❖ A piece of chewing gum stuck under the dinner table will one day return to haunt you.

❖ Never hold a dust buster and a cat at the same time.

❖ The only time the world beats a path to your door is when you're in the bathroom.

❖ Never spit while you're riding a roller coaster.

❖ A bird in the hand makes blowing your nose difficult.

❖ Always carry an umbrella – you're guaranteed it won't rain if you do.

❖ Never buy a DVD player in the street from a man who is out of breath.

❖ The best way to serve cabbage is to someone else.

❖ Don't sneeze when someone is cutting your hair.

❖ Never tell a lie unless it is absolutely convenient.

❖ The best way to forget all your troubles is to wear tight shoes.

❖ Never buy a car you can't push.

❖ Always wear a hat when feeding seagulls.

❖ Never dare your younger brother to paint the family car.

❖ Don't take life too seriously. Nobody gets out alive anyway.

Old enough to know best

Grandfatherly advice can sometimes seem rather dubious, but children can always rely on Grandad to know best – or to *think* he knows best...

FIRST IN LINE

Harmonica player Larry Adler claimed that his grandfather changed the family name from Zelakovitch because he didn't want to be last in the queue when he emigrated from Russia to the United States.

LIFE AND DEATH

A family was celebrating Katie's sixth birthday at a local restaurant when the little girl's grandfather noticed her looking sadly at a moose's head mounted on the wall. Someone had placed a party hat on its head.

Kneeling down next to her, Grandad gently explained why some people hunt animals.

'I know all that, Grandad,' answered Katie, 'but why did they have to shoot him at his birthday party?'

THE BIRDS AND THE BEES

Grandad was looking after his nine-year-old grandson one evening when the boy suddenly asked, 'Grandad, I know that babies come from mums' tummies, but how do they get there in the first place?'

Shocked at being asked such a forthright question, Grandad hummed and hawed while trying to think of a suitable response. Eventually his grandson said bluntly, 'You don't have to make something up, Grandad. It's okay if you don't know the answer.'

Lessons in life

Not all grandfatherly advice is of the smart-alec kind, however. Grandad's age and life experience make him the ideal person to turn to in times of trouble or confusion, as these heart-warming stories show.

TELLING IT ALL

Since 2006, an English grandfather-of-two calling himself Geriatric1927 – a reference to the year he was born – has become an internet sensation by virtue of

'Telling it All', a series of short autobiographical videos broadcast on YouTube.

Peter Oakley's gentle stories about his life – including his World War Two exploits and his love of motorcycles – have earned him over five million fans from around the world. He has made more than 200 videos, the nature of which he describes as 'like fireside chats with friends', and attracts a sack full of fan mail that would be the envy of most pop stars. America's *Time* magazine has called him a 'superstar'. His many followers praise his 'grandpa-like' style of storytelling and he has been hailed as the 'coolest old dude alive'. Another fan wrote simply, 'I wish you were my grandfather.'

In a recent interview, Peter said he derived particular satisfaction from the fact that his videos are such a hit with young people.

'Mainly they are surprised that someone of my age can and would do such things and liken me to their own grandparents, who would not consider even using a computer. So in this respect they think I am "cool".'

> 'I keep a lot of opinions to myself. My grandfather, who was a gravedigger, told me one day: "Son, the next time you go by the cemetery, remember that a third of the people are in there because they got into other people's business."'
> LEE TREVINO

TARZAN'S WISDOM

When Tarzan creator Edgar Rice Burroughs became a grandfather to Danton around the time of the D-Day landings in 1944, he decided to write his grandson a letter welcoming him to the world. He wanted his grandson to read the letter on his twenty-first birthday in 1965.

'If your generation shows more intelligence than past generations,' wrote Burroughs, 'perhaps there will be no more wars. But that is almost too much to expect. See [in 1965] if the politicians have kept your country great and strong. If they haven't, do something about it. If I'm around I'll remind you.'

Edgar Rice Burroughs did not live to see Danton read the letter, but he left a strong impression on his grandson nonetheless.

'My grandfather led the life of few individuals,' said Danton. 'He had tremendous energy and drive. But he was also such a good family man, so down to earth. He was an amazing man.'

> 'My grandfather [Motilal Nehru] once told me that there are two kinds of people: those who work and those who take the credit. He told me to try to be in the first group; there was less competition there.'
> INDIRA GANDHI

TWO WOLVES

A Cherokee elder was teaching his grandchildren about life. He told them, 'A fight is going on inside me. It is a terrible fight between two wolves. One wolf represents fear, lies, anger, envy, resentment, sorrow, regret, greed, arrogance, self-pity, guilt, false pride and superiority. The other wolf stands for joy, peace, love, hope, sharing, serenity, humility, kindness, benevolence, friendship, sympathy, generosity, compassion, honesty and faith. This same fight is going on inside you, and inside every other person, too.'

His grandchildren thought about what he had said

and then one of them asked, 'But Grandfather, which wolf will win?'

'The one you feed,' replied the old man.

> *'My Bampy is so wise. He's the coolest man on earth, like Dumbledore.'*
> CHARLOTTE CHURCH

In the kitchen with Grandad

GRANDMA MAY BE the undisputed boss in the kitchen but, being a modern grandad, you like to show that your skills extend beyond opening the lids of stubborn jars or popping a ready-cook meal into the microwave. The perfect chance to display your full culinary repertoire comes when you are on babysitting duty. Then, for one night only, you can forget the healthy option and make your grandchildren something you know they'll love.

Cooking for children

Cooking for your grandchildren can be rather a daunting prospect. After all, children are creatures of habit; how are you to know the nuances of what they like and don't like, or how they're used to having things cooked and served? Even something as innocuous as an unwelcome vegetable or the 'wrong' salad dressing can have them refusing point-blank to eat anything. Help!

KEEP IT SIMPLE

As is so often the case with children, keeping things simple really will make mealtimes more harmonious. Here are some things you might consider when planning what to cook for your grandchildren:

❖ DON'T try anything new or fancy – children aren't gourmet diners; they're just hungry.

❖ DO ask their parents in advance what they will and won't eat, and if there's any special way in which things need to be prepared.

❖ DON'T serve up a meal whose constituent parts aren't easily recognizable. Children don't take well to unidentifiable objects concealed by gravy.

❖ DO tell the children what you're planning on cooking, to check for any violent reactions.

Grandad's favourite recipes

As a grandad, you'll no doubt have mastered a handful of traditional recipes that are quick, easy and delicious – the sort of things you cook for yourself when home alone. The good news is that these are exactly the kind of simple meals that children enjoy, too.

TOAD IN THE HOLE

This dish is perfect for grandads and grandchildren: quick, cheap and incredibly simple – and with a delightfully yucky name that's guaranteed to make the children laugh.

Serves 2

INGREDIENTS

1 packet batter mix
1½ tbsp sunflower oil
2–3 sausages per person, depending on hunger levels
Greens of your choice to serve

METHOD

1. Make the batter mix according to the instructions on the packet, following the directions for Yorkshire pudding rather than pancakes.

2. Put the oil in an ovenproof dish and place in the oven at 200°C (Gas Mark 6).

3. While waiting for the oil to heat up, gently grill or fry the sausages for about 10 minutes, turning them from time to time.

4. Once nicely browned, put the sausages into the ovenproof dish, pour the batter mix over them, and cook the whole lot for a further 20–25 minutes until the batter is risen and golden.

5. Serve with green beans, peas, carrots or broccoli so that your grandchildren can tell their mum they've had plenty of vegetables.

> 'What children need most are the essentials that grandparents provide in abundance. They give unconditional love, kindness, patience, humour, comfort, lessons in life – and, most importantly, cookies.'
> RUDOLPH GIULIANI

SHEPHERD'S PIE

A real 'Grandad' dish that's inexpensive, relatively easy to make, and will warm you all up on a cold winter's day.

Serves 4

INGREDIENTS

> 900g potatoes, peeled and chopped into
>   manageable chunks
> 1 tbsp oil
> 1 onion, chopped
> 450g minced beef or lamb
> 300ml (½ pint) beef stock
> Salt
> 50g butter
> 2 tbsp milk
> Grated cheese

METHOD

1. Bring the potatoes to the boil and let them bubble away for 20 minutes, until soft.

2. Meanwhile, heat the oil in a frying pan and cook the chopped onion for a few minutes, stirring constantly.

3. Add the mince to the pan and cook for a few more

minutes – long enough for all the meat to brown –
and break up the mince with a wooden spoon as it is
cooking.

4. Add the stock and a little salt and leave to simmer
   for about 20 minutes.

5. Once the potatoes are cooked, mash them and stir
   in the butter, milk and some seasoning.

6. Spoon the mince into a casserole dish and spread
   the mashed potato on top. With a fork, rough up the
   surface of the mashed potato a little so that it crisps
   up nicely when cooked.

7. Sprinkle some cheese on the mashed potato and
   bake in the oven at 200ºC (Gas Mark 6) for about
   30 minutes, until the potato is golden brown.

Cooking with children

Cooking *with* children – with them helping you, that
is, not using them as ingredients – is a whole world
of anxiety away from simply cooking *for* them. While
children absolutely love to get involved with cooking,
particularly when there's a chance of making an
enormous mess, there are a few things to bear in mind

before letting them loose with the chopping board:

DO be clear about how you would like them to help, and show them how it's done.

DON'T let them do anything involving knives without very careful supervision.

DO involve them in every stage of the preparation, even if they are only watching you. Learning how meals are prepared is a great lesson for children.

DON'T let them anywhere near a hot oven or hob, unless they are a little older and you know that they will be careful.

Recipes to cook with children

Rules and regulations aside, cooking with children is great fun for all involved. Children are often more inclined to try a new taste when it is part of a dish they have made themselves, so turn the dinner preparation into a group activity and you'll have nothing but empty plates to clear away at the end of the meal.

GRANDAD'S SPECIAL PIZZA

What makes Grandad's Special Pizza so special? Well, it's never the same thing twice! Start off with the same base each time but let your grandchildren dictate – within reason – what goes on top. With their endless permutation of toppings, pizzas present the ideal opportunity to introduce your grandchildren to the likes of mushrooms, salami, peppers, pineapple, olives, spinach, onion and anchovies.

Tip: If your grandchildren can't agree on a topping, don't let them waste valuable cooking time arguing about it! Simply allocate a half or a third of the pizza to each child and let them take responsibility for their own section.

Each pizza will serve 2–3 people, depending on hunger.

INGREDIENTS
> *1 ready-made pizza base*
> *Tomato paste*
> *Mozzarella cheese*
> *Toppings of your grandchildren's choice*

METHOD
1. Since life is too short to make your own pizza base,

buy a ready-made one and then brush it with olive oil before smearing it with tomato paste.

2. Sprinkle on a layer of grated mozzarella cheese.

3. Get creative with the toppings, bearing in mind that those of a soft consistency will produce the best results (no raw carrots, no chocolate-chip cookies).

4. Once perfectly adorned, stick the pizza into an oven preheated to 220° (Gas Mark 7) and bake for 15–20 minutes, until the base is browning around the crust and the toppings have melted together.

BANANA SPLIT

It looks good, it tastes good, and, when Grandma complains about you feeding the children a bowlful of ice cream and cream, smugly remind her of the nutritional fruit content.

Serves 1 very greedy child (or grandad)

INGREDIENTS
   1 banana
   2 scoops ice cream
   A few squirts raspberry or strawberry sauce

¼ can spray cream
Hundreds and thousands or chocolate chips

METHOD

1. Peel the banana and cut it in half lengthways, and then arrange the halves in a dessert bowl.

2. Plop a couple of scoops of your grandchild's favourite ice cream between the banana halves.

3. Squirt the raspberry or strawberry sauce over the ice cream and squirt some cream down the sides.

4. Finally, sprinkle hundreds and thousands or chocolate chips on top.

Grandad the inspiration

WHILE PARENTS MEAN to inspire their children to achieve great things, there is something about the grandad-grandchild bond that provides an even stronger inspiration for an impressionable child. Perhaps it's the lack of antagonism inherent in that relationship that makes children want to emulate their grandparents instead – if Grandad can do no wrong, why not aspire to be like him?

Manilow in Manhattan

Barry Manilow's grandfather was a Russian immigrant who, for most of his life, supported Barry, his mother and his grandmother.

'I'll always be grateful to him for that,' says Barry, 'but the other reason I'll never forget him is because he was the first person in my family who actually noticed that I was a musical kid.'

There were precious few clues because the family couldn't afford any musical instruments but, as Barry says, 'Somehow Grandad just got it. On Saturday afternoons he used to take me over the Brooklyn Bridge into Manhattan to a little record-your-own-voice booth that he'd found. It cost a quarter, which was a lot of money then. He put his quarter in and he tried to get me to sing – anything. I remember he tried to get me to sing "Happy Birthday" to my cousin Dennis, but I just wouldn't.'

After half an hour or so of trying, Grandad gave up, but continued with his efforts every Saturday afternoon, and eventually his persistence paid off when Barry sang something for him – and realized how much he enjoyed it.

'Years later,' says Barry, 'when "Mandy" got to number one, I played Carnegie Hall and I invited everyone I knew, including my family. And Grandad was there in the audience. When I walked out on stage, scared to death, Grandad stood up and gave me a standing ovation and because he stood up, the whole audience stood up, so I got my first big standing ovation. And when they sat down, he wouldn't sit down – he just kept standing there and applauding. I looked at him and my fear just vanished because I knew what he was thinking: "There's my grandson on the stage of Carnegie Hall, down the block from that twenty-five-cent record-your-own-voice booth!'"

'That's for you, mate!'

When Australian cricketer Andrew Symonds scored his first Test century against England in Melbourne in 2006, he dedicated it to the memory of his grandfather, who had died twelve weeks previously. On reaching his ton – on the way to a majestic innings of 156 – Symonds embraced batting partner Matthew Hayden, looked to the heavens and mouthed four words: 'That's for you, mate.'

Adopted at birth, Symonds doesn't know his blood grandfather but Tony Hemming represented the next best thing.

'Whenever I play in Melbourne I save a thought for him,' says Symonds. 'The old man loved his cricket and every time I played in Melbourne he would be there. He was the grandfather who did everything for me. As a kid, he was the one who bought me ice cream and lollies. When I turned eighteen, he bought me my first beer and we'd sit at home and talk about life and cricket … That's why that knock against England meant so much to me. It was for my grandad.'

'Every generation revolts against its fathers and makes friends with its grandfathers.'
LEWIS MUMFORD

Dumpy grandad

Veteran golfer Arnold Palmer may be 'Arnie' to his legions of fans, but to his grandchildren he is 'Dumpy'. It has nothing to do with his waistline, but is merely the result of a mispronunciation by his granddaughter Emily. As his grandson Sam explains, 'When she was young, she'd try to say "grampy" or "grumpy" but it came out "dumpy". It stuck. The world knows him as "Arnie" or "The King" but to us he'll always be "Dumpy".'

A promising young golfer in his own right, Sam has learned a lot from his legendary grandad.

'His philosophy,' says Sam, 'is "Be humble, and don't act like you're better than anyone. When you meet someone, look them right in the eye, and let them know you're interested in them as a person."'

At the age of sixteen, Sam had the honour of caddying for his grandfather at the 2004 US Masters – Palmer's fiftieth and final appearance at the tournament.

'It was one of the greatest times of my life,' said Sam afterwards, 'to see how much respect people have for him, and how much he appreciates it. If he wasn't my grandfather, I'm sure I'd still think he was a great guy.'

George and Lilibet

King George V was not exactly renowned for his love of children, but he made a notable exception for his granddaughter Elizabeth, who subsequently became Queen Elizabeth II. He doted on her and the feeling was mutual. On Christmas Eve 1928, two-year-old Princess Elizabeth was allowed to stay up late to listen to the carol singers, and when she heard 'Glad tidings of great joy I bring to you and all mankind', she called out excitedly, 'I know who Old Man Kind is!' It seemed only natural to her that people should sing enthusiastically about her grandfather.

The royal household observed how enthusiastically the king played with his granddaughter – something he had never done with his own children. He would pretend to be a pony so that she could ride on his back and he would even encourage her to pull his beard. He called her 'Lilibet', imitating her own attempts at saying her name. The name stuck, and she became Lilibet to her family from then on. She in turn called him 'Grandpapa England', because he had told her that the national anthem, 'God Save the King', was his song.

When they were in the countryside together, the king would take Elizabeth to see his collection of horses, and he presented her with her first pony, a Shetland called Peggy, for her fourth birthday in 1930.

George's fervent hope was that, one day, his darling Lilibet should be queen. When his eldest son Edward VIII abdicated to be succeeded by Elizabeth's father, Grandpapa England's dying wish eventually came true.

Musical genes

Ludwig van Beethoven inherited his musical genes from his grandfather Ludwig, who during the eighteenth century had served as Kapellmeister to the Elector of Bonn, a post that put him in charge of all of the city's official musical activities. Although Beethoven hardly knew his grandfather, who died when young Ludwig was just three, he let it be known that he greatly revered the man and throughout his life kept a portrait of him in his house.

Cricket and composition

Although Don Bradman made his name as one of the world's greatest cricket batsmen, he was also an accomplished pianist and composer. It was his passion for music that inspired his granddaughter Greta Bradman, now regarded as one of Australia's finest young singers.

As a young girl in Adelaide, Greta went to her grandparents' house every day after school. There, Bradman would often play the piano while Greta danced around or sang. On other occasions, they would listen together to his vast collection of LPs.

'He'd sit me down,' she recalls, 'and I'd have to listen properly to this music, and we'd talk about what I'd heard and what I was keen on.'

Her chance to acknowledge his musical tuition came in 2008 at a dinner to mark the 100th anniversary of his birth (Bradman had died in 2001). At the dinner, Greta sang one of Bradman's compositions, 'Every Day Is a Rainbow For Me', published in 1930. Afterwards she said, 'It was lovely being able to sing something Grandpa had composed.'

> *'My grandfather taught me generosity. He sold snow cones in Harlem. I went with him at five and he let me hand out the change and the snow cones. I learned a lot in the couple of years that we did that.'*
> ERIK ESTRADA

I know what I like

GRANDADS ARE LOVABLE rogues and wonderful companions – but they can't half be stubborn! If things aren't done in the good old-fashioned way, Grandad will let everyone know about it. Central heating? Put on an extra jumper! Bored? Make your own fun!

Grandads don't suffer fools gladly, and aren't afraid to put their foot down and mutter – all together now – 'It wasn't like this in my day!'

> 'My grandfather told me long ago that if you haven't got anything good to say, don't say anything.'
> LEE WESTWOOD

Grandadisms

Every grandad will have his own set of trademark phrases, but, as these real-life stories prove, there are dozens of grumpy sayings, cynical mottos and downright rants that grandads the world over seem to share.

YOU CAN LEAD A HORSE TO WATER...

British broadcaster and chat show host Michael Parkinson says that, although his miner grandfather Sammy lived into his mid-seventies, he never took his family on holiday and never visited London.

Sammy did once go to Leeds, walking the thirty miles there and back, to see Don Bradman play cricket for Australia, but his only other excursion was a bus trip to Blackpool with the local working men's club. He was so disappointed with the beer across the border in Lancashire that he had just one pint and started walking back home to South Yorkshire!

Don't suffer fools gladly

Grandad was driving with his seven-year-old granddaughter as a passenger, when he sounded the horn by mistake. She immediately turned and looked at him for an explanation.

'I did that by accident,' he said.

'I know that, Grandad,' she replied.

'How did you know?' he asked.

'Because,' she said, 'you didn't shout "Idiot!" afterwards.'

CHILDREN SHOULD BE SEEN AND NOT HEARD

King Edward VII was well known for his indulgence to small children, but it was severely tested one day when he was having lunch with his son, the future George V, and his four-year-old grandson, the future Edward VIII.

While the king was speaking, the little boy suddenly cried out, 'Grandpa!' Firmly but fairly, he was told not to interrupt adults. However, a moment later, he called out again – more urgently this time – 'Grandpa! Grandpa!'

'You must not speak while I am speaking,' the king

told him patiently. 'When I have finished speaking, you will be allowed to say what you wish.'

After a few minutes, the king did indeed finish speaking. True to his word, he turned to his grandson to ask him what it was that he wanted to say.

'I was going to tell you there was a caterpillar on your lettuce,' the boy replied. 'But it doesn't matter – you've eaten it.'

ASK A SILLY QUESTION...

One day, Ashley decided to introduce his eighty-six-year-old grandfather to the magic of the internet. Opening a popular reference website, Ashley told Grandad that this site was so clever it could answer any question he asked.

'I don't believe it,' replied Grandad sceptically.

'No, it's true,' insisted Ashley. 'Think of something to ask it and then just type in your question on the keyboard.'

As Ashley watched with eager anticipation, Grandad slowly typed: 'What are we having for dinner tomorrow?'

DON'T LOOK A GIFT HORSE IN THE MOUTH

'I have many lovely memories of my grandad,' says comedian Dawn French, 'a very powerful one being his eccentric obsession with bargains. If he found out that something, anything, was going for a song, he'd find a reason to get there and snaffle up the bargain, whether it was something he needed or not. Hence, for years, he had two pairs of enormous department-store front doors leaned up against his shed. He had no use for them as far as I knew, he'd just got them for a good price.'

Len also used to go to jumble sales and pick up stacks of ties. Eventually, he had collected so many ties that he had to move them out of the house and into his caravan.

'Pretty soon,' says Dawn, 'it was impossible to get into the caravan.'

NOTHING IS BUILT TO LAST ANYMORE!

Having bought a new Ford Thunderbird in 1955, Grandad continued to drive it for the next fifty-five years. One day, he was driving his grandson to the airport when it started to rain. He switched on the windshield wipers but they merely caused the drops of rain to smear across the screen, effectively worsening visibility.

Disgusted, Grandad moaned, 'Nothing is built to last anymore!'

His grandson nodded sympathetically and asked, 'When did you buy the wipers?'

Grandad looked at him, confused, and said, 'They came with the car.'

> 'My grandfather always told me that the only thing worse than a door-to-door salesman was two of them.'
> ANON

IT WASN'T LIKE THIS IN MY DAY

The curmudgeonly observations of a seventy-three-year-old grandfather on the social networking website Twitter went down a storm in 2009, with more than 50,000 people signing up to read his comments on society in the first three months alone. The anonymous blogger laid into everything from celebrities to answering machines in a typically 'grumpy old man' manner.

His greatest bugbear would appear to be modern

technology: 'Why would I want to check a voicemail on my cell phone? If people want to talk to me, call again. If I want to talk to you, I'll answer.'

Another choice tweet tackled health foods: 'I didn't live to be seventy-three years old so I could eat kale.'

More grandadisms

Here are some more phrases from the unique language of grandads that may sound familiar:

❖ When I was a lad…

❖ I used to have to walk ten miles to school every day through snow up to my knees.

❖ Look after the pennies and the pounds will take care of themselves.

❖ I can't be doing with all this metric stuff.

❖ I can remember when this was all fields.

❖ Of course your mother won't mind.

❖ What's that in proper money?

❖ How much?!

❖ We were poor but happy.

- ❖ What's the matter? Cat got your tongue?

- ❖ There's always someone in the world worse off than you.

- ❖ Some days you're the pigeon, and some days you're the statue.

- ❖ You call that music?

- ❖ If we clean everything up quickly, Grandma need never find out.

The world's most stubborn grandad?

Sixty-two-year-old grandad Roy Locock drove 39,000 miles round the world to prove a point – just because someone had casually told him that his classic car would never make it.

Roy had bought the 1977 MG Midget (named Bridget) on impulse, and was restoring it at his Oxfordshire home in 2008 when a friend asked him what he was going to do once the work was finished.

'I said I was going round the world and, rather jovially, he said I couldn't. Things were going wrong that morning. I kept banging my hands with the hammer and that kind of thing, so I said I would prove him wrong.

And thirteen weeks later, I was on my way.'

His sixteen-month journey saw him delayed by floods in Australia and by two earthquakes in Panama. He was also driven off the road by a tanker in India and woke up to the sound of a Taliban rocket attack in Pakistan. His family never worried about the dangers involved.

'They said if that's what I wanted to do, then I should do it. They know I'm slightly crazy.'

Where was I?

A TYPICAL 'GRANDAD' characteristic that goes hand-in-hand with his stubbornness is his bafflement at the modern world. Gadgets, instructions, new-fangled rules and regulations – these are not things that grandads enjoy.

But who cares? Modern life is becoming more modern and confusing every day, so why not revel in your right to lose your glasses, forget your children's names and birthdays, and wilfully mishear everything?

'I used to be with it – then they changed what "it" was. Now what was it isn't it, and what is it is weird and scary to me. It'll happen to you, too.'
GRAMPA SIMPSON

Confusing capers

If you're starting to fear that your memory isn't quite what it once was, you will perhaps take heart from these true stories of grandfatherly mystification.

APPLAUSE! APPLAUSE!

Attending a meeting of a literary society in Paris with his grandson, Benjamin Franklin was confused when a series of colourful compliments were exchanged in French. Unsure as to precisely what was being said, he decided to clap only when a lady of his acquaintance also applauded.

Afterwards, he bemoaned his difficulties with the French language.

'But Grandpapa,' said his grandson, 'you always applauded – and louder than anyone else – when they praised you!'

LUCKY LAPSE

A shortsighted grandad from Roanoke, Indiana, won a $3m lottery jackpot in 2008 because he forgot his bifocals.

Bobby Guffey usually plays the same combination of numbers – representing the birthdays of his five children – but on this occasion he left his glasses at home and accidentally entered the final number as 48 instead of 46. He said he would use his winnings from the Hoosier Lotto to set up a trust fund for his five children and ten grandchildren.

'My wife says it pays to be blind,' he added.

> *'I come from a long line of completely impractical people. My grandfather used to Scotch-tape carpet to the stairs.'*
> ELVIS COSTELLO

MYSTERY TOUR

Eighty-one-year-old grandfather Eric Steward drove for nine hours and over 600km after setting off early one morning in November 2009 to buy a newspaper.

The former navy seaman had been on his way to a shop near Canberra, Australia, where he and his wife were staying with friends, but he took a wrong turn and just kept on driving – all the way into the next state, beyond Melbourne. When he found himself in Geelong, he finally stopped at a service station and asked a police officer to contact his wife.

When asked why he hadn't stopped for directions eight hours ago, Eric simply answered that he enjoyed driving.

'It didn't worry me,' he said of his unscheduled detour. 'I just thought, with a bit of luck, I will eventually find my wife again, which I did.'

Asked whether he would consider buying a GPS, he replied, 'Why would you want one of those? You can't get lost. There's no fun in that.'

Stay-at-home grandad

For Grandad's one-hundredth birthday, there was a huge family celebration and even a picture of him in the local paper.

'That's a nice shot of you,' remarked his grandson.

'It's my passport photo,' said Grandad, proudly.

'You have a passport photo?' said the grandson, amazed at the thought of his grandfather travelling anywhere out of the country. 'Where did you go?'

'The post office,' replied Grandad.

THE GRANDAD WITH MORE THAN NINE LIVES

A sixty-seven-year-old Scottish grandfather has suffered no fewer than nine brushes with death. John Watt has accidentally shot himself twice, survived two car crashes, run himself over, cut through a live mains cable while gardening, been hauled out of a river and a harbour, and had a slate crash through the sunroof of his car, missing his head by inches.

John, from Aberdeenshire, Scotland, says the most embarrassing incident was being run down by his own car.

'I had a flat battery and was parked at the top of a hill. I pushed it and when it started rolling, I went for the driver's door but that was locked for some reason. So I ran round the front of the car, which was a really stupid thing to do. I couldn't get away from it and it hit me. I was pinned between it and a shop.'

After that incident, John enjoyed a few trouble-free years until the 2009 episode with the slate.

'Everyone has mishaps and accidents,' he adds ruefully, 'but I suppose I've had more than most people. I just hope I've not pushed my luck too far. I want to be around for a while longer – I'm about to be a great-grandad for the first time.'

> 'My grandfather's a little forgetful, but he likes to give me advice. One day, he took me aside and left me there.'
> RON RICHARDS

Quiz: Are you a crazy grandad?

Give grandads an audience of adoring grandchildren and they'll completely forget that, at their age, they're supposed to be intelligent, rational adults. Instead, they will react to any unexpected obstacles in the way their grandchildren have come to love and expect – that is, with mock befuddlement and comic eccentricity.

Try this quiz to see whether you fall into the category of 'Crazy Grandad'.

1. There is no room in your wheelie bin for one last bag of trash. Do you:

a) Save the excess bag until the next collection;

b) Use your hands to press down firmly on the trash bags already in the bin;

c) Climb into the wheelie bin and jump up and down manically, squashing everything with your feet?

2. You are enjoying a family picnic on the beach when the incoming tide suddenly sweeps your ham sandwich out to sea. Do you:

a) Watch forlornly as your lunch disappears out to sea;

b) Jump up and down on the beach in a display of mock rage;

c) Dive fully-clothed into the sea, retrieve the soggy sandwich and then eat it?

3. You are on a trip to the zoo with your grandchild when the male gorilla rushes over to the front of his enclosure and starts beating his chest aggressively right in front of you. Do you:

a) Back away and take your grandchild to see another animal;

b) Say, 'I think he wants to get something off his chest';

c) Beat your own chest wildly and make gorilla noises back at him?

4. You are baking a cake with your granddaughter when some of the mixture accidentally splashes up on to your face. Do you:

a) Wipe it off with a cloth;

b) Try to lick it off with your tongue;

c) Flick some of the mixture at your granddaughter and start a full-scale messy food fight?

5. An uninvited salesman knocks on the door of your house. Do you:

a) Ignore him and hope he will go away;

b) Open the door and try to sell him some worthless item of your own;

c) Bark loudly like a large dog and scratch at the door from the inside, in the hope of scaring him off?

If you've answered mainly c), you are without a doubt a Crazy Grandad!

If you've answered mainly b), you're certainly well on your way to full-blown quirkiness – keep it up!

If you've answered mainly a), come on, Grandad – let your combover down and embrace eccentricity!

Crossed wires

In the course of a hospital check-up, Grandad was given a urine sample container and told to fill it up in the bathroom. A few minutes later, he returned to the nurse with an empty cup.

'I didn't need this after all,' he said. 'There was a toilet in there.'

Daredevil grandads

THEY SAY WISDOM comes with age, but an increasing number of modern grandads are railing against the idea of being 'past it', choosing instead to travel the world, throw themselves out of aeroplanes and generally embrace life-threatening pursuits – all in the name of fun…

> 'If wrinkles must be written upon our brow, let them not be written upon the heart; the spirit should never grow old.'
> JAMES A. GARFIELD

Celebrity daredevils

If you're looking for inspiration for your next daring and death-defying act, take some encouragement from these celebrity grandads.

HOLLYWOOD ROYALTY

Suzanne Lloyd spent the first twenty years of her life living with her grandfather, silent movie comedian Harold Lloyd. In the early 1960s, when Suzanne was about nine and didn't quite understand her grandfather's day job, Harold took her to Cannes to see a preview of a compilation of his short films, which he had just edited.

'I was sitting in front of him,' recalls Suzanne. 'The film starts, and there is this clip of a guy climbing a building. They said it was my grandfather. I didn't think it looked like him. But it was really odd. Some of his smiles and expressions were like his. He was sitting right behind me and I kept turning around. Afterwards the press asked, "Weren't you just petrified that your grandfather was hanging out of a building?" I said, "No, I kept turning around and he was OK."'

Harold Lloyd's daredevil approach extended even to his more sedate hobby, photography. He thought nothing of marching out into busy traffic or climbing up San Francisco's Golden Gate Bridge simply to get a better shot.

'He just did crazy things,' laughs Suzanne.

Competitive streak

American international hurdler Jenny Adams believes she inherited her competitive nature from her grandfather. She says, 'He is so competitive that whenever he mows the yard, he wears a stop watch around his neck to time himself and comes in all excited because he broke his personal record!'

LIKE GRANDFATHER, LIKE GRANDSON

While Formula 1 driver Lewis Hamilton races around a track at 200mph, his paternal grandfather Davidson drives a 15mph school bus on the Caribbean island of Grenada. But it wasn't always so. After passing his test in 1947, Davidson used to roar around the island on his BSA motorbike, once astounding locals by covering the three treacherously bumpy miles between his home and the next village in just five minutes.

'I was known as the fastest thing on wheels around here,' smiles Davidson. 'I used to tear up the roads but I never had an accident. Then I got an Austin A40 car and got stopped for speeding.'

Davidson is tremendously proud of his grandson's achievements and has flown over to Europe to watch Lewis race in Grand Prix races.

'He is a very nice young man who is respectful and thoughtful when it comes to the welfare of others. He takes pride in his ability at speed, but I take equal pride these days in driving the children to school safely. But I still tell Lewis he inherited his speed from me!'

Real-life recklessness

If tales of celebrity hell-raising haven't put you off being a daredevil grandad, check out these real-life stories. Perhaps a nice quiet cup of tea and a sit-down is a good idea, after all.

ROLLERBLADES OF GLORY

A seventy-year-old grandad who regularly skated around a Lancashire town in the middle of the night became an unlikely internet star in 2007. The Rollerblade Grandad Appreciation Society website contained video footage and photographs of Jeff Dornan rollerblading outside local landmarks, and soon attracted more than 1,000 members.

Jeff explained, 'I have a health-conscious daughter and when I turned sixty-four she started nagging me about doing exercise. I signed up to the gym but only went once. She was telling me to do power walking but I just found it so boring that I knew I wasn't going to keep it up. I remembered when I was seventeen I used to ice skate and loved it. So I started rollerblading, and in six years of skating I have not had a single significant collision with anybody. That's why I go out at night – during the day there's so many old people getting in the way!'

ON YER BIKE

In 2007, Scottish grandad Robbie Allan became the oldest-ever competitor to tackle the infamous 5,000-mile Dakar Rally from Paris to Senegal – on a motorcycle. His granddaughter Megan said, 'I don't think any other grandads can do motorcycling at sixty-seven. He can hardly walk, but he cycles for miles. I can't even do that, and I'm thirteen!'

HIGHFLIER

Eighty-eight-year-old grandad Tom Lackey was named the UK's number one young-at-heart pensioner in 2008 after completing seventeen wing walks, having taken up flying in 2000 following the death of his wife.

'It's something I've always wanted to do and every time I go up in the skies I take a picture of my wife with me so that she's there next to my heart and is flying with me. Mind you, if she was alive today and knew I was wing walking, she'd probably kill me!'

The grandfather-of-two has raised more than £1 million for charity and, in 2005, achieved a world record as the oldest man to perform a loop-the-loop while strapped to a bi-plane.

'My family think I'm mad,' admits Tom, 'but I think they're pleased I live life to the full.'

HELL'S GRANDAD

In 2005, sixty-eight-year-old grandad Keith Parnell rode a high-powered 1200cc Kawasaki motorbike at a speed of 199mph in speed trials on the runway of a former US air base in Suffolk. He competed against riders who weren't even born when he got his licence in 1958. Afterwards Keith confessed, 'It does get a bit harder to hang on at that speed when you get older.'

Gifts for a daredevil grandad

Daredevil grandads are the last people in the world who'd derive any sort of pleasure from traditional 'Grandad' gifts such as slippers, cardigans or pipes. Today's young-at-heart grandad is just as likely to be taking flying lessons or planning a solo voyage across the Atlantic.

Since a sixty-foot catamaran may be out of your price range, here are a few alternative gift ideas for the grandad whose get-up-and-go hasn't yet got up and gone:

❖ An iPod will allow Grandad to listen to all
   his favourite music while he jogs, walks or tries

desperately not to hear Grandma's demands that he help with the washing up.

❖ A Nintendo Wii will enable Grandad to get plenty of exercise without having to step out of his house – from boxing to snowboarding to F1 driving. He might let you play, too, so long as you don't beat him.

❖ With racetrack gift vouchers, Grandad will be able to realize his dream of being Michael Schumacher – instead of someone permanently stuck behind a caravan on a narrow country road – by driving a real racing car around a racetrack.

❖ Forget the waltz and the foxtrot: modern grandads prefer to strut their stuff to a funkier rhythm. Salsa dancing lessons will prove that you can indeed teach an old dog new tricks.

❖ A compact camcorder will allow Grandad to film his favourite grandchildren having fun together – or allow Grandma to film Grandad abseiling off the nearest cliff.

❖ Skiing lessons are a great way of enjoying the fresh air – provided Grandad can still bend his knees.

❖ A personalized crystal whisky glass inscribed 'To The

World's Bravest Grandad' will make his post-exercise medicinal drink all the more pleasurable.

> 'I wish I had the energy that my grandchildren have – if only for self-defence.'
> GENE PERRET

Traditional games with Grandad

OF COURSE, WHEN you were a lad, there were no computers and TVs so – as you never tire of telling people – you had to make your own entertainment. This probably involved playing traditional outdoor games such as hide-and-seek or tag, which usually ended with you covered in mud and tearing your best school shirt.

Nevertheless, they were happy days, so why not resurrect some of these simple, long-forgotten games to play with your grandchildren in the garden or at your local park?

Some traditional games

Teaching your children traditional outdoor games is a great way of bonding with them, and you'll be surprised how quickly they forget about the computer games and DVDs lurking indoors. And the best thing about these games is you don't need any equipment – just plenty of energy.

SWING THE STATUE

One player is chosen to be 'it'. He or she then takes each of the other players in turn by the hand and swings them round before letting go. The swung player must freeze immediately and hold that position – no matter how uncomfortable – for as long as possible. The first player to twitch or move becomes 'it', and you start all over again.

You can continue playing this game until the dizziness becomes permanent.

> *'The simplest toy, one which even the youngest child can operate, is called a grandparent.'*
> SAM LEVENSON

WHAT'S THE TIME, MR WOLF?

One player is chosen to be the wolf and stands facing away from the others, who line up about ten metres away. They then call out, 'What's the time, Mr Wolf?' and the wolf turns round and shouts a time, for instance seven o'clock. The players take the corresponding number of steps (in this case, seven) towards the wolf.

When the wolf turns away again, they repeat, 'What's the time, Mr Wolf?' If the wolf says it's four o'clock, they move four steps forward.

The wolf only faces the others when calling out the time, but, as the players get closer and call out 'What's the time, Mr Wolf?', the wolf senses his moment and suddenly growls back, 'It's dinner time!'

The players run back – generally screaming – to the start line as fast as they can, but the first player caught before reaching the line becomes the wolf for the next round.

This is a fun, boisterous game but it is probably best not played with any child who has a phobia of wolves.

SIMON SAYS

While one player is 'Simon', the others stand in a straight line. Simon then calls out an action for the others to follow – maybe 'touch your toes three times' or 'scratch your head'.

Whenever the instruction is prefixed with the words 'Simon says...', it must be obeyed. But any player who performs the action when there is no 'Simon says...' prefix has to sit down and is out of the game. The last person standing is declared the winner and becomes Simon next time round.

With the right orders, you can burn off more calories with this old favourite than at an aerobics class.

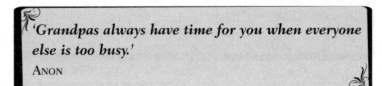

'Grandpas always have time for you when everyone else is too busy.'
ANON

RED LIGHT, GREEN LIGHT

One person is designated as 'it' and plays the part of the stop light. The other players line up about twenty feet away. With his or her back to the other players, 'it' calls out 'Green light', whereupon they start to creep closer. 'It' then calls out 'Red light' and turns around quickly. Any of the players who are caught moving must go back to the start line. Play continues until someone reaches and tags 'it', at which point that person becomes 'it'.

If you are playing the game with a mixture of ages, in the interests of fairness let the youngest start closer.

'My grandfather [actor Lon Chaney, Jr.] ... would say, "Let's play cards", and then teach us how to play gin rummy. He also loved wrestling and boxing and used to wrestle with us on the grass. He was always a lot of fun to be around. We were always excited to go down and see him, to just be around him, because he had that kind of personality.'
RON CHANEY

The outdoor adventurer

WHETHER OR NOT you have any actual experience or expertise in the field of outdoor adventure, your grandchildren will automatically assume that you do. Grandads, after all, grew up in the age of Oliver Twist and no running water, and presumably had to catch their own dinner – or so grandchildren think.

Embracing this adventurous persona when you're around your grandchildren is easy – simply choose an intrepid sport and invent a children's version. They need never know you haven't a clue what you're doing!

Planning your adventure

For a young-at-heart grandad, few prospects are as exciting as that of spending a day or two with their grandchildren. There are limitless possibilities for an unforgettable adventure. Take into account your grandchild's age, confidence level and phobias, and suggest something new and exciting you can explore outdoors. These real-life stories and anecdotes might provide food for thought...

FISHING

In 2008, fifty-six-year-old David Hayes of North Carolina used his granddaughter's pink Barbie fishing rod to land the biggest catfish ever caught in the state.

David and his three-year-old granddaughter Alyssa were fishing with the toy rod at a pond behind his house. Alyssa asked her grandad to hold the rod while she went back to the house – only to return to find him struggling with a fish so big that it threatened to break her rod.

After a twenty-five-minute wrestle, Grandad was finally able to show off a monster twenty-one-pound catfish, which, at thirty-two inches in length, was two inches longer than the rod!

DEEP-SEA DIVING

'My grandfather inspires me in everything that I do,' says Alexandra Cousteau, an environmentalist and the granddaughter of legendary marine explorer Jacques Cousteau. 'As you can imagine, coming from the Cousteau family, water has always been an important part in my life. I learned to swim before I learned to walk, I first went on an expedition when I was four months old, and I started diving with my grandfather when I was seven. He taught me about the oceans and showed me the importance of living a life of consequence, value and meaning.'

HUNTING

Grandad used to work in a grocer's store that had an old stable yard at the back. Lying around in the yard was an old, battered, fifty-six-pound lead weight that was missing its handle.

'What's that for, Grandad?' asked his young grandson.

'Catching rabbits, lad,' replied Grandad.

'How do you catch rabbits with that?' asked the boy.

'Place it in the centre of the room,' explained

Grandad, 'cover it with lettuce leaves and some pepper, and when the rabbits come to eat the lettuce and get pepper up their noses, they sneeze and knock themselves out. In the morning, I just pick them up.'

The boy scratched his head.

'But ... I've never seen any rabbits in here.'

'Caught 'em all, lad!' said Grandad with a grin.

MOTOR RACING

Nominating her grandad, Robert Hatton from Middlesex, for Age Concern's Grandparent of the Year 2009 award, Lizzie Thomson said he is the perfect hands-on grandad with a great sense of fun: once, when his car was blocked in after a trip to the shops, he wheeled his granddaughters home in a supermarket trolley.

> *'A grandpa is only old on the outside. He's young on the inside.'*
> ANON

BOBSLEDDING

Travel writer Bill Bryson has fond memories of times spent with his grandparents at their home in Iowa. His grandad had a Model T Ford, which he allowed the children to drive around the yard; in winter, he would attach a sleigh to the back and take them for rides along the snow-covered roads.

> 'Grandchildren don't stay young forever, which is good because pop-pops have only so many horsey rides in them.'
> GENE PERRET

Rules for a successful camping trip

Camping is one of life's simple pleasures, but it's so easy to forget something vital. If you're planning a longer trip rather than a simple camp in the back garden, close to the luxuries of a bathroom and fully stocked fridge, check off these easy do's and don'ts and you should be guaranteed a stress-free few days in the open air.

DO...

❖ Remember to pack a tent – and a sturdy one at that.

❖ Bring a cooking stove and fuel, tins of food and bottles of water.

❖ Remember to pack a tin opener.

❖ Take a couple of layers of clothing in case the weather suddenly changes.

❖ Pack insect repellent, particularly if you are camping near water.

❖ Take a fully-charged mobile phone, just in case you need to summon assistance – or are desperate for some grown-up conversation with Grandma or your friends.

DON'T...

❖ Pitch your tent on low-lying ground that is prone to flooding.

❖ Pitch your tent in any field that bears the sign 'Beware of the Bull'.

❖ Forget your map.

❖ Forget the camp leader's motto: loo roll, loo roll, loo roll.

Rainy-day adventures

If your proposed adventure is a washout, perhaps you can adapt your plans along the lines of these indoor exploits:

❖ Wear safari hats and khaki clothes and explore a museum of natural history, you doing your best David Attenborough impression as you sneak up on the animals.

❖ Spend a few hours in the water slides and wave machines of your nearest child-friendly swimming pool, imagining you are Indiana Jones and his sidekick on the run from a band of baddies.

❖ Camp inside the house instead of in the garden, using sheets draped over the backs of sofas and chairs to build your camp. Ghost stories and a midnight feast will still be mandatory.

❖ Depending on your own bravery and your grandchild's age, book a couple of hours' indoor climbing lessons at a sports centre. If you don't fancy scaling walls yourself, you could always arrange for your grandchild to do so while you watch.

❖ If all else fails, watch an adventure movie at home with some exotic snacks and drinks.

Grandad's magic

As a GRANDAD, it's vital to have a number of tricks up your sleeve – quite literally – to whip out at the first sign of restlessness, boredom, tantrums or tears in your grandchildren. There are few things guaranteed to impress children more than magic tricks, and who better than Grandad to light up their eyes with a baffling demonstration of sleight of hand?

Grandad's top 10 magic tricks

Young children are the best audience for simple magic tricks, as they won't even think to shout, 'Show me how you did it, Grandad!' They'll simply watch in awe as you prove once again that grandads are simply amazing.

But remember to keep to simple, harmless tricks. Do not get too ambitious: you are not a master illusionist and there is just a chance that your grandchildren may become upset if you announce that you are about to saw Grandma in half.

THE AMAZING SUGAR CUBE

YOU WILL NEED
> A *sugar cube*
> *Assorted colouring pens*
> A *jug of water and a glass*

METHOD

1. Ask your grandchild to draw a big dot on one side of the sugar cube, using the coloured pen of his or her choice. Make a big show of turning your back so that you can't see which colour they've chosen.

2. Ask your grandchild to place the sugar cube colour side down on a table, before turning around to begin the trick.

3. Make an elaborate play of telling your grandchild that you will now read his or her mind to work out which colour they chose. Meanwhile, pour some water into the glass, taking care to dampen your right thumb as you do so, and place the glass to one side.

4. Pick up the sugar cube, still number side down, with your right forefinger at the top and your right thumb at the bottom. Press your moistened thumb firmly against the coloured base of the cube, allowing the dot to transfer onto your skin.

5. Look intently into your grandchild's eyes as you move the sugar cube over to the glass of water and nonchalantly plop it in.

6. As it dissolves, ask your grandchild to hold up the coloured pen they used, and proudly hold up your thumb to reveal the same colour.

Tip: Should your grandchild wish to emulate your amazing talent, swap roles and carry out the trick as before – but casually instruct them to pick the cube up by its sides rather than by the top and bottom. This way, the colour won't transfer onto their skin and you can maintain your magical mystique!

ROPE TRICK

You will need

A piece of string about 30cm long

Method

1. Before starting the trick, tie a knot in one end of the string, out of sight of your audience.

2. Hold the knotted end of the string in your hand so that nobody can see it, and then bring the other end of the string up next to it and close your fingers around both ends.

3. Announce that you will now tie a knot in the string using just one hand.

4. Say a magic word, blow on your hand and release the knotted end of the string to tumultuous applause.

BOTTOMS UP

You will need
A deck of playing cards

Method

1. Before you begin, secretly turn the bottom card of the deck face upward.

2. Fan out the cards in your hand, face down, making sure you don't show the rogue end card, and invite your grandchild to pick a card.

3. When the card has been chosen, close the deck and switch it into your other hand, in the process turning the deck over so that the odd card is now face down on the top.

4. Ask your grandchild to remember the selected card and to insert it into the middle of the deck.

5. If you think you can get away with it, make some distracting banter while you quickly turn the bottom card back the right way, and then fan out the cards to reveal your grandchild's chosen card, which by now will be the only one facing the wrong way.

6. Alternatively, turn your back on your audience 'to concentrate on isolating the right card' and fan open the cards in your hand. Your grandchild's chosen card will be the only one, apart from the top card, which is facing the wrong way.

TRIANGLE OF COINS

You will need
  10 coins

Method

1. Arrange ten coins in a triangle – one at the top, two on the second row, three on the third row and four at the bottom.

2. Ask your grandchildren whether they think it is possible to turn the triangle upside down by moving only three of the coins. They might try or fail or simply say it's impossible. That's when you say you will show them how it's done.

3. Move the top coin down to a position below the middle two coins on the bottom row. Then move the coin at either end of the original bottom row up two rows and, hey presto, you have created an inverted triangle.

THE VANISHING COIN

YOU WILL NEED
> A *small coin*
> A *large handkerchief with a hem – you may have to*
> *fashion this yourself*

METHOD

1. Before starting the trick, secretly slip a small coin into the handkerchief's hem.

2. Loudly ask someone (your son or daughter) if you can borrow a coin of the same denomination as the one you have hidden in the handkerchief, saying you will use it for a trick.

3. Holding the folded handkerchief in your right hand and the borrowed coin in your left, pretend to wrap the coin somewhere in the middle of the handkerchief, but instead hide it in your left hand in the fleshy area between the base of your thumb and your forefinger.

4. With the handkerchief still folded over, ask your grandchild to feel that the coin is safely wrapped inside. He or she will, of course, feel the one hidden in the hem and assume it is the borrowed coin.

5. Grandly announce that you will make the coin disappear.

6. Whip one corner of the handkerchief through the air and hold up both sides for everyone to see. The coin is still tucked safely in the hem but the handkerchief will appear to be empty. As far as your audience is concerned, the coin has vanished!

'My Hungarian grandfather was the kind of man that could follow someone into a revolving door and come out first.'
STEPHEN FRY

THE MISSING CARD

YOU WILL NEED
   A deck of playing cards
   A child-friendly glue stick (e.g. Pritt stick)

METHOD

1. Before beginning your trick, take a deck of playing cards and smear the four edges of the back of the top card with glue.

2. Announce that you are going to make a card disappear completely from the deck.

3. Fan the cards out, face down, and ask your grandchild to select a card from somewhere in the middle of the deck, and to show it to everyone else in the room except you. While they are showing the card, collect up the remaining cards – ideally without gluing your hands together.

4. Take the card from your grandchild and, without looking at it, place it face down on top of the deck, casually pressing it down onto the sticky back of the card beneath, so that they form one card.

5. Cut the deck a few times and deal out the cards face up. Making sure you handle the glued cards carefully, show everyone that the chosen card has indeed vanished – just as you had promised.

MATHEMATICAL GENIUS

YOU WILL NEED
> *Two pieces of paper*
> *An envelope*
> *A pencil*

METHOD

1. Announce that you are going to use your special magical powers to predict which random number your grandchild will write.

2. Ensuring that your grandchild can't see what you're doing, write down a four-figure number that is exactly twice the sum of the current year. So in 2010, you would write 4020.

3. Fold the piece of paper and ask your grandchild to place it into the envelope without looking at it. Seal the envelope.

4. On another piece of paper, ask your grandchild to write down the answers to the following four questions:

   ❖ His or her year of birth

   ❖ The year of an important event in his or her life, such as starting school

❖ The number of years since that important year

❖ His or her age at the end of this current year

5. Ask your grandchild to add up the four numbers (with young children, you will probably have to ask Mum or Dad to help). The total will always be twice the current year.

6. Ask your grandchild to open the sealed envelope, and the number inside will be the same as the number they have randomly generated.

COLOUR BLIND

YOU WILL NEED
   A box of assorted coloured wax crayons

METHOD
1. Place a box of assorted coloured wax crayons on a table and turn your back so that you can't see them.

2. Ask your grandchild to take a crayon from the box, saying that you will be able to guess correctly which colour has been chosen.

3. Ask your grandchild to hand you the selected crayon behind your back.

4. Turn round to face your grandchild, with the crayon still held behind your back, and announce that you are feeling it for inspiration. What you are actually doing is digging your right thumbnail into the wax.

5. Still keeping the crayon out of sight behind your back, use your right arm to gesticulate that your grandchild must really concentrate on the crayon's colour so that it can be transferred to your mind. While you're doing this, glance at your thumbnail to see which colour the wax is.

6. Craftily flick off the wax and correctly name the colour. Magic!

'I became interested in magic at an early age. I learned a card trick from my grandfather when I was seven, which involved four aces. Each time I perform that trick in a show is a special tribute to his memory.'
DAVID COPPERFIELD

SNEAK PEEK

YOU WILL NEED

A deck of playing cards

METHOD

1. Ask your grandchild to select any card from the deck and then tell him or her to show it to everyone else in the room apart from you.

2. While everyone's eyes are on the chosen card, glance down at the bottom card in the deck and remember it.

3. Ask your grandchild to put the chosen card back on top of the deck, face down, without showing you.

4. Cut the deck somewhere in the middle and square it off neatly so that it is clear that there is no chicanery in the form of a protruding card.

5. Fan out the cards, face up. The chosen card will be the one on top of the one you glanced at earlier.

6. Hold up the chosen card and milk the applause.

MAGIC NUMBER

You will need
> *Three dice*
> *A pencil*
> *A piece of paper*

Method

1. Hand your grandchild three dice, a pencil and a piece of paper.

2. With your back turned, ask your grandchild to stack the three dice on top of one another.

3. Ask your grandchild to add up the numbers on the five hidden faces – i.e. the bottom face of the top dice and the tops and bottoms of the other two dice – and to write the total on a piece of paper.

4. Ask your grandchild to hide the slip of paper somewhere out of your view.

5. Turn round, glance quickly at the dice and boldly announce the number on the hidden paper.

How on earth does this work? It's simple: the opposite faces of a dice always add up to seven, and therefore the opposite faces of *three* dice add up to twenty-one. All you have to do is look at the number on the upper face of the top dice and subtract it from twenty-one. So if the top face shows a three, the five hidden faces must total eighteen.

And that's magic!

What a gentleman!

WITH AGE COMES wisdom – and also a profound understanding of 'the done thing'. Grandchildren the world over, from every walk of life, invariably describe their grandads as true gentlemen – people who always do the decent thing and go out of their way to be polite and respectful.

'My grandfather came from Brazil and he was a very attractive man. He had a sort of elegance, this dark air, and he was also very gentle. He would take me on his bike. He was the best grandfather. A prince.'
CLAIRE DENIS

Tact and decorum

When it comes to true gentlemen, few figures from recent history can quite match Winston Churchill, whose granddaughter Celia Sandys describes as a warm person and a wonderful companion.

'I wasn't interested in politics at that age,' she remembers, 'so we'd be more likely to talk about whether his horse had won the latest race or where he'd painted that afternoon.'

Celia says her grandfather loved to share his pleasures.

'If he was drinking champagne, he wanted everyone else to drink champagne. When I was about fifteen, there was an elderly cousin who complimented my mother on her daughter – that was me – and then went for the kill: "Pity the child drinks so much!"'

One of Celia's favourite stories about her grandfather concerns a formal dinner in Virginia. When the butler came around with the chicken and asked Churchill which piece of the bird he would like, Churchill replied, 'I'd like breast.' Hearing this, the woman seated next to him said, 'Mr Churchill, in this country we say white meat or dark meat.' The next day, the woman received a corsage of flowers with the message, 'Pin this on your white meat!'

On the day of his state funeral in 1965, Celia travelled with her grandfather's coffin on its final journey through the streets of London.

'He was a lovely grandfather,' she says. 'He still casts a ray of summer on the family.'

Secret president

Clifton Truman Daniel was six years old before he learned that his grandfather, Harry S. Truman, had been president of the United States. He simply knew him as 'Grandpa Truman', so that when a school friend asked him, 'Wasn't your grandfather president of the United States?' Clifton replied with disarming honesty, 'I don't know.' Even after he had prised the information out of his mother, she told him, 'Just remember. Any little boy's grandfather can be president of the United States. Don't let it go to your head.'

Clifton describes his grandfather as 'the last truly accessible ex-president'. After retiring, a casually dressed Harry S. Truman answered a knock at his door one morning. The stranger standing there asked to use the phone because he had a flat tyre.

'Sure,' said Truman, 'Come on in.'

The stranger phoned for a mechanic who said

there would be a twenty-minute wait. Clifton says his grandfather insisted that the man make himself comfortable and the pair chatted in the living room until the tow truck arrived.

'The man then shook Grandpa's hand and thanked him for his hospitality. "Not at all," Grandpa said, showing the man out. "It was nice talking to you." The man got halfway down the front steps before he stopped and turned. "I hope you won't take offence," he said. "But you look a lot like that son of a bitch Harry Truman."

'"No offence at all," said Grandpa with a wide grin. "I *am* that son of a bitch."'

The world's most charming bouncer

In 2009, great-grandfather Eric Voyce was still working as a bouncer at the University of Wales social club in Cardiff, aged ninety. Eric had stepped in twenty-five years previously when the regular doorman failed to turn up for work, and he continued to report for duty three nights a week from 5pm to 11pm thereafter.

One of the barmaids described him as 'a real gentleman', adding, 'If anyone has any problems, he'll sort them out.'

Eric, who has dealt with drunks and violent soccer fans in his time on the door, said, 'I'm as fit as a fiddle and can cope with any problems. I'd like to carry on until I am 100.'

As one respectful punter commented, 'Only gentlemen make good doormen.'

> '*My grandfather was a wonderful role model. Through him I got to know the gentle side of men.*'
> SARAH LONG

In Nelson's shadow

To one young man growing up in South Africa, the family name was just something that was shouted on the streets during protests. Mandla Mandela, eldest grandson of Nelson Mandela, says, 'I grew up with the name "Mandela", but it never had a meaning to me. I didn't attach it to my grandfather until the first time I visited him with my grandmother in Pollsmoor Prison. I thought he was a criminal. It was only later that I realized he was fighting for the liberation of his people.'

Mandla says that, despite his enforced absence from the family, his grandfather always encouraged his grandchildren to study.

'He was strict and insisted on discipline, but he was also the kind of grandfather every child would dream of. He told us tribal stories about him growing up. He has taught us about our heritage and where we've come from.'

Now a politician in his own right, Mandla proudly acknowledges his grandfather's work.

'There won't be another Nelson Mandela. My grandfather has astounding achievements and has created a huge legacy for the Mandelas. We strive to hold onto a small piece of that, to do something to honour him.'

Cricket's grand old man

Sir Pelham Francis Warner – known affectionately as 'Plum' – captained the England cricket team in the early years of the twentieth century before becoming one of the game's leading administrators and chroniclers. He was often referred to as 'the grand old man of English cricket'.

His eldest granddaughter, novelist Marina Warner, remembers him living in a South Kensington flat full of cricketing memorabilia, including a clock in the shape of a wicket, a clothes brush in the shape of a bat, and a cigarette box in the shape of a ball. He was of slim build with an appetite to match; one evening at dinner when asked if he would like a second helping, he replied, 'One pea, please.'

Marina says her grandfather's 'self-effacing yet poised, slender and impressive figure embodied history for me, not only a chapter of cricketing history, but also many loops and knots to do with England and abroad, with ideas about where one belongs and who one is: he was the pattern of an English gentleman.'

Talking, talking, talking

'My grandfather [George Lansbury] was an extraordinary figure in British politics,' recalls actress Angela Lansbury. 'He was a Socialist and founded the Labour Party in Britain in the early 1900s. He was beloved by the people and the workers of England. He went from north to south, from east to west, talking, talking, talking, trying to better the lot of the working man.

'He was a wonderful speechmaker; he spoke at Hyde Park Corner and we as children were taken to hear him. I remember hearing him in the Albert Hall in London. I was absolutely awed by his delivery and the way he controlled the crowd. That was one of the things that I realized I would have loved to have been able to emulate – to make a speech like he did and grab the imagination and the enthusiasm of the crowd. And he did it like nobody I ever heard in all my life.

'It did have a definite effect on me as a kid. I would go home and give speeches. I inherited his voice, thank God, because it enabled me to do big roles later in my life and never have any problems with my voice – it always held out for me – and I think I got that from him.'

'The thing with my grandfather [John Wayne] was, he really walked the walk that you saw in his characters onscreen. He lived his patriotism and believed in doing the right thing in the toughest moments, and I think people sensed that in how they embraced him. He wasn't just an actor but an example, and somebody who impacted people's lives in a profoundly positive way.'
BRENDAN WAYNE

Perfect grandad checklist

YOUR GRANDCHILDREN OBVIOUSLY think you're the world's greatest grandad – they gave you this book, didn't they? – but are there any traditional 'Grandad' areas you could improve in?

> 'A grandpa is someone you never outgrow your need for.'
> ANON

What makes a great grandad?

This top 10 checklist of true Grandad qualities will help you rate yourself as a grandad. The more you can tick off, the more perfect you are!

1. BRUTALLY HONEST

Brad Pitt recalls the occasion when he telephoned his grandparents and his grandfather said, 'We saw your movie.'

'Which one?' asked Pitt.

His grandad shouted, 'Betty, what was the name of that movie I didn't like?'

'I thought that was just classic,' laughs Pitt. 'I mean, if that doesn't keep your feet on the ground, what would?'

2. PROUD

When the grandchildren of comedy writer and actor Eric Sykes discovered that he did other things besides being a grandad, Sykes was, as he put it, 'elevated to the ranks of stardom by my only, but most important, treasured fan club.' Young Thomas and Sophie recognized his voice on the TV introducing the popular children's programme *Teletubbies* and were totally astounded.

In his autobiography *If I Don't Write It Nobody Else Will*, Sykes described how, shortly afterwards, Thomas's school class was asked to name famous people. After fellow pupils had suggested Winston Churchill and Florence Nightingale, Thomas put his hand up and announced, 'My grandad's famous!' Consequently, wrote Sykes proudly, 'my name was chalked on the board underneath two of the most revered people in our history, for which honour I thank my little grandson.'

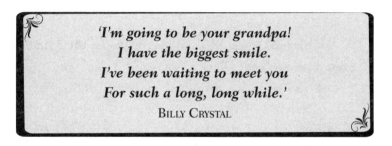

'I'm going to be your grandpa!
I have the biggest smile.
I've been waiting to meet you
For such a long, long while.'
BILLY CRYSTAL

3. DIGNIFIED

American journalist and TV anchorman Nick Clooney – father of actor George and brother of singer Rosemary – has warm memories of his grandfather Andrew, a self-made man who taught himself to read and write Greek and who 'was very funny and very stubborn'. Andrew

153

Clooney was once mayor of Maysville, Kentucky, where he was responsible for the building of an important bridge, the opening of which drew a huge crowd and was attended by numerous dignitaries including the then US secretary of state, Harold Dickey.

Like both Nick and George, Grandad Clooney had prematurely grey hair. He thought he was far too young to go grey, so he decided to put black shoe polish on his hair, which had the unfortunate effect of turning his hair bright purple. For the big celebration, he concealed his embarrassment with a straw hat, forgetting that he would have to take it off for the playing of 'The Star Spangled Banner'.

'There he stood,' remembers Nick, 'all 6ft 2in, and stared at everyone, daring someone to say something about his hair being purple.'

Playful pull

Five-year-old Harry had always been fascinated by his grandad's moustache and loved to give it a gentle, playful tug. One day he asked him, 'Grandad, what's so special about your nose that it's got to be underlined?'

4. OLD AS THE HILLS...

A little girl was sitting on her grandad's knee while he read her a story about Noah's Ark. After he had described how Noah led the animals, two by two, to the safety of the Ark, the little girl asked, 'Grandad, you're very old. Were you in Noah's Ark?'

'No, sweetheart, I wasn't,' laughed Grandad.

'In that case,' said his granddaughter, suddenly concerned, 'how come you didn't drown in the flood?'

5. ...BUT YOUNG AT HEART

Grandad was telling a friend about the seniors' fitness class he had recently joined.

'Goodness, that's very energetic of you,' said the friend. 'How did it go?'

'Well,' said Grandad, 'I twisted, I turned, I jumped up and down, and I perspired for an hour – but by the time I'd finally got my leotard on, the class had ended!'

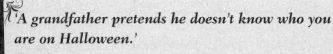

'A grandfather pretends he doesn't know who you are on Halloween.'
ERMA BOMBECK

6. ECCENTRIC

Simon Tolkien's first memory of his grandfather, *Lord of the Rings* author J.R.R. Tolkien, is of playing a game called Grandmother's Footsteps in the garden of his house near Oxford. Grandad Tolkien would stand on the lawn in his velvet waistcoat, puffing on his beloved pipe while young Simon crept up on him.

'I am four or five and I'm really scared,' he recalls. 'He is huge, with a great roar in his voice, and he's coming to get me. I am just about to cry when I see the twinkle in his bright eyes, and realize it's all just fun.'

Simon recalls his grandfather being inseparable from his pipe – even though the only time he ever inhaled was by accident, when he was riding his bicycle and the wind was against him.

> '*My grandfather told me about senility, I'm not worried about that. My grandfather said, "When you become senile, you won't know it."*'
> BILL COSBY

7. CHARMINGLY CHEEKY

Cockney actress Barbara Windsor owes much of her enthusiasm for show business to her Grandad Ellis, who used to appear on stage at drinking clubs in London's East End billed as 'The Versatile Comedian'. He delighted in sitting young Barbara down and telling her stories about the music hall and expressed a hope that one day she, too, would go on the stage.

'Grandad Ellis was the epitome of a Cockney man,' she wrote in her autobiography *Barbara*. 'Hard-working, warm-hearted, witty and generous, too, despite the poverty he'd known most of his life.'

He used to work at the docks from early morning until lunchtime, pop into the pub and stagger home just as Barbara was coming out of school.

'Mummy told me I must walk on the other side of the road and ignore him. She didn't like me seeing him tiddly. He'd sing songs like "My Ol' Man" and "Are Soles Lovely". Mummy hated anything coarse. I always waited for him, though. He'd give me tuppence to buy a jam doughnut or threepence for a quarter of sherbet lemons, my favourites.'

8. UNDER GRANDMA'S THUMB...

George had been his own family's doctor for more than thirty years, so his young grandson Ben was surprised to be taken to a different doctor.

'Why aren't we going to see Grandad?' he asked.

His mother explained, 'Because Grandad has retired.'

'What's retired?' asked Ben.

'That's when Grandad can do anything he wants.'

'No, he can't,' protested Ben. 'He has to do what Grandma tells him!'

9. ...BUT SECRETLY A REBEL!

Actor David Hemmings' grandfather Percy was a master carpenter.

'He made wonderful furniture and drank Guinness by the bucketload,' wrote Hemmings admiringly in his autobiography *Blow-Up and Other Exaggerations*. 'His balding head with its halo of drifting white hair was a source of wonder to me, and I loved the smell of wood shavings and the way he gently pushed a chisel across the surface of a block of mahogany, his hands flowing over the wood like a snake charmer's.'

The morning's work done and the tools cleared away, however, Grandad would produce a secret bottle of Guinness from a pile of sawdust and drink the contents with relish. As they prepared to go back to the house, he would turn to the boy and warn him sternly, 'Don't you go telling Grandma about the stout!'

> *'On the seventh day God rested. His grandchildren must have been out of town.'*
> GENE PERRET

10. QUICK-WITTED

Grandad was among a group of American senior citizens travelling on a bus tour through France's Loire Valley. Stopping at the village of Chavignol, they visited a farm where the world famous Crottin de Chavignol goats' cheese is made. The farmer's wife acted as tour guide and took them through the entire process of cheese making, revealing the subtle differences between goats' milk and cows' milk.

She then showed the group a beautiful hillside where goats could be seen grazing peacefully. These, she explained, were the older goats put out to pasture when they no longer produced.

'Tell me,' she said with national pride, 'what do you do in the USA with your old goats that aren't producing?'

Grandad piped up, 'They send us on bus tours.'

> 'The idea that no one is perfect is a view most commonly held by people with no grandchildren.'
> DOUG LARSON